CAUGHT IN THE CROSSFIRE

Helping Christians Debate Homosexuality

Edited by

Sally B. Geis &
Donald E. Messer

ABINGDON PRESS / Nashville

CAUGHT IN THE CROSSFIRE
Helping Christians Debate Homosexuality

Library of Congress Cataloging-in-Publication Data

Caught in the Crossfire : helping Christians debate homosexuality / Sally B. Geis and Donald E. Messer, editors.
    p. cm.
    Includes bibliographical references.
    ISBN 0-687-09524-7 (alk. paper)
    1. Homosexuality—Religious aspects—Christianity. I. Geis, Sally B., 1928– . II. Messer, Donald E.
BR115.H6C38   1994
241'.66—dc20   93-33341

99 00 01 02 03—10 9 8 7 6

To
Ann and Porter Brown, M.D.,
Kent D. Messer, and
Christine M. and Gordon P. Gallagher

CONTENTS

Contents

ACKNOWLEDGMENTS

Acknowledgments

As we prepared this book under the pressure of many responsibilities and quick deadlines, the paraphrased poetry of William Butler Yeats came to mind: "Count where our glory most begins and ends, and say our glory was we had such friends." Without the incredible connection of colleagues across this country, the manuscript could have taken neither form nor substance.

The splendid cooperation and contributions of the various authors who submitted essays for this volume need to be underscored. Even when sharply dissenting with each other, they demonstrated the Christian art of disagreeing in love. They strongly supported this project aimed at helping the church debate homosexuality and willingly wrote and sometimes rewrote their chapters to meet the space limitations of this book. We owe an enormous debt of gratitude to Richard and Catherine Clark Kroeger, Victor Paul Furnish, Ruth L. Fuller, Joseph Nicolosi, Marva J. Dawn, James B. Nelson, Richard C. Looney, Tex S. Sample, Chris Glaser, Riley B. Case, and Larry K. Graham.

At various stages in the editing process, we called upon a vast array of friends to help us identify possible contributors, find needed bibliographical material, critique manuscripts, and test the value and viability of this style of book. The people on the following list bear no responsibility whatsoever for the final product, but they do deserve a tremendous "thank you" from us for their gracious counsel and assistance at various points:

Edwin Boulton, Mark Bowman, Delwin Brown, Robert McAfee Brown, Scott Daniels, Maxie Dunnam, Christine M. Gallagher, Robert B. Geis, Bettina Harmon, Richard Hays, Roberta Hestinez, Rachel Julian, Elinor Lewallen, Dennis R. MacDonald, Joretta Marshall, Bonnie J. Messer, Paul Millette, Albert "Fritz" Mutti, Julian Rush, David Seamands, Richard Simons, Christine M. Smith, Sylvia Thorson-Smith, Timothy Weber, Mary Wilcox, Joan Winfrey, and Philip Wogaman.

Suzanne Calvin provided invaluable expertise in editing, and our able assistants, Virginia White and Alberta Smith, proved to be secretaries par excellence. Along with Gene Crytzer and Revel Loedy they were indispensable in completing this manuscript in a timely fashion. Likewise, we would be remiss indeed if we failed to express our appreciation to The Iliff School of Theology for providing us a place where such issues can be freely explored and scholarship is encouraged.

CONTRIBUTORS

Riley B. Case currently serves as senior pastor of St. Luke's United Methodist Church, Kokomo, Indiana. His published curriculum materials include *We Believe,* a confirmation resource for junior highs and adults, and *Handbook on Biblical Prophecy,* published by Good News. He is also the author of a religious column in *Hobart Review.*

Marva J. Dawn is Director of Christians Equiped for Ministry, Vancouver, Washington. She has served as a Christian educator in a number of settings and as organizer of the Inter-Lutheran Task Force on Ministry to Single Adults. Her most recent publication is *Sexual Character: From Technique to Intimacy.*

Ruth L. Fuller is Associate Professor of Psychiatry, University of Colorado Health Sciences Center. She is a member of the American Psychoanalytic Association, a member/examiner for the American Board of Psychiatry and Neurology, former Director of Mental Health Clinics for East Harlem, New York, and an elder in the Presbyterian Church U.S.A.

Victor Paul Furnish is University Distinguished Professor of New Testament, Perkins School of Theology and 1993 President of the Society of Biblical Literature. He is an ordained elder in The United Methodist Church, and his numerous books include *The Moral Teachings of Paul: Selected Issues, Theology and Ethics in Paul,*

Corinthians II in the Anchor Bible Commentary Series and *Jesus According to Paul.*

Sally B. Geis is Director of the Iliff Institute for Lay and Clergy Education at The Iliff School of Theology and a member of the clinical faculty of the Department of Psychiatry, University of Colorado. A United Methodist laywoman, she served on the United Methodist Committee to Study Homosexuality. Her articles on homosexuality, grief, and AIDS appear primarily in scientific publications.

Chris Glaser, while studying at Yale Divinity School, served on the Presbyterian Task Force to Study Homosexuality. He is author of *A Gay Man's Struggle to Serve the Church, Come Home! Reclaiming Spirituality and Community as Gay Men and Lesbians,* and a book of prayers entitled, *Coming Out to God—Prayers for Lesbians and Gay Men, Their Families and Friends.*

Larry Kent Graham is Professor of Pastoral Theology and Care at The Iliff School of Theology and a Diplomate in the American Association of Pastoral Counselors. He serves on the editorial committees of numerous pastoral care journals. His most recent book is *Care of Persons, Care of Worlds: a Psychosystems Approach to Pastoral Care and Counseling.* He is ordained in the United Church of Christ.

Catherine Clark Kroeger is a ranked Adjunct Associate Professor of Classical and Ministry Studies at Gordon Conwell Theological Seminary and has served as a teacher of Biblical and Classical Greek at the University of Minnesota. She and her husband are authors of *I Suffer Not a Woman: Rethinking I Timothy 2:12 in the Light of Ancient Evidence.*

Richard Clark Kroeger, Jr., is Director of the Cape Cod Institute of Bible and Christian Studies. He has served as a Presbyterian pastor and teacher of religion in various settings. His film pro-

useful to productive group decision making than abstract, theoretical religious conversations.

Second, dialogue depends upon mutual understanding and mutual trust. If one's goal is to overcome misunderstanding and develop or preserve friendships in the face of conflict, it is wise to choose gentle, healing words rather than sharp, hurtful ones during the discussion. Too often, persons seem eager to find faults or question motives or integrity of others. Sometimes questions are raised not to learn but to embarrass, confuse, or harass others. Those who take pleasure in winning need to remember that creating losers in a Christian dialogue can lead only to greater conflict and more distrust.

Third, dialogue makes it possible to share in service to the community. Dialogue is not a secret weapon or a propaganda tool; it is a way to remove barriers and reduce tension among persons so that divisions can be transcended and the church can be about its mission to the world.

Fourth, dialogue becomes the medium of authentic witness. Dialogue happens to promote honest understanding of differences. If we cannot be honest with each other, how can we truly love each other?[5]

Honesty, not Compromise

Readers closely identified with one inflexible position or the other in the homosexuality controversy may be distressed to discover the format of this book, as well as the methodology we suggest for its use, encourages informed study, reflection, and discussion rather than divisive debate in which one side wins. On the other hand, they may be heartened to know each chapter presents material from contrasting points of view, so the conflict of disagreement is not minimized. It is, however, placed within the context of "speaking the truth in love," as mandated for Christians, lest we be "tossed to and fro and blown about by every wind of doctrine, by people's trickery, by their craftiness in deceitful scheming" (Eph. 4:14).

Our format is risky because the danger inherent in presenting "sides" in an educational context is that the technique has a tendency to polarize or even politicize the perspectives of persons who read the material.[6] Polarization in discussion is unfortunate because most church study groups will discover many members who do not identify completely with either end of the opinion spectrum. After discussing the chapter on the Bible or the one on science, many persons will be left with a deeper understanding of the difficulty of translating words in scripture from one language to another or of interpreting research data collected on a small number of subjects. A deeper appreciation for the problem does not always result in the development of a altered conclusion about what the Bible says or what science proves.

Rather, exposure to a diversity of opinions within the group promotes deeper appreciation of one's own position as well as a better understanding of others. One study group we know included a visit to the home of a gay couple as part of the study experience. After spending an evening at dinner with the couple and hearing their story, one conservative, evangelical woman said to her study group, "Well, I still believe it's a sin. But for heaven sakes, it's not the *only* sin. Now that I've met these men and shared a meal with them, whenever I read in the paper about a gay who's been beaten or killed in our city I'm going to have to wonder, 'Was he somebody I know?' " This woman's insight is a kind of response we hope to evoke. She broadened her perspective and deepened her understanding.

We urge each study group to develop a covenant among its members encouraging each member to listen carefully and nonjudgmentally to the comments of others. A simple list of rules may be useful, for example:

1. Stipulate that only one person speaks at a time.
2. Recommend that listeners ask themselves, Am I really listening, or am I using the time to formulate my rebuttal?
3. Allow no name-calling.
4. Focus on one subject at a time.

5. Watch for inflammatory language. "Shoulds and oughts" sound judgmental and tend to be self-righteous. Never say never.

6. Avoid mind reading. Ask a person, "Did I hear you correctly? Is this how you are feeling? Is this what you are saying?"

7. Use descriptive words with care. Conservatives and liberals sometimes use different words to discuss same-sex orientation. Language used to describe any minority or powerless group in society is frequently more inflammatory than some speakers realize. For example, calling women "girls" or African-American men "boys" is offensive. How do persons of same-sex orientation feel about being called homosexuals? gays? ex-gays? Why do some persons take offense at the word *homophobia*?

Developing a set of group rules such as these, and attempting to follow them, allows *all* persons within the group to express opinions and share personal experiences without fear of being contradicted or ridiculed by others. In the end persons with deeply held but different convictions may be able to say to each other in love and sincerity, "I do not agree with you, but now I understand why you feel as you do."

When an atmosphere of flexibility and freedom prevails, unexpected commonalities may emerge within a group that initially seems quite polarized. On the other hand, asking study groups to reach watered down consensus is not our goal. Robert Wuthnow suggests, "Differences need not be run through a blender of debate to create some gruel that neither side finds palatable. Ways of maintaining and encouraging respect for diversity need to be set up. At the same time, there may indeed be common ground worthy of exploration."[7]

T. M. Scanlon describes yet another technique for maintaining the integrity of diverse opinions while discerning areas of agreement in his review of Ronald Dworkin's work on a different controversial issue:

What [is asked] of us, as participants in the . . . debate, is not compromise but honesty . . . [the book] offers us an account of our own values and challenges each of us to judge the accuracy of this account, to look for counter examples, and to come up with better accounts if we can.[8]

Individual readers of this book are invited to attempt this difficult process. Challenge the accuracy of your position by trying to dismantle the arguments of authors with whom you *agree* rather than authors with whom you disagree. Those who understand the weak points in their arguments are in a better position to understand opposing arguments as well as possible points of agreement between the two. The most productive disagreements develop when each side's position is clearly understood by everyone.

Can We Do Better?

Will traditional mainline denominations survive the current ideological turmoil over homosexuality? Or will the pain, anger, and frustration of liberals and conservatives alike become so great that the foundation of love, trust, and respect necessary to hold a community of faith together be eroded beyond repair?

A recent poll suggests few Americans express mild opinions about their approval or disapproval of homosexuality. Most expressed strong convictions on one side or the other, and many relied on their religious convictions to back their opinions.[9] The same poll reports 46 percent of respondents do not know anyone who is gay but are opposed to gay rights.

Many are irritated because they believe the church is spending too much time and money on a nonissue. They resent being called homophobic and believe that if we quit talking about homosexuality in the church, it will go away or back to wherever it was before we made such a fuss over it!

In such a hostile climate it may not be possible for persons within local churches or denominational bodies to hold reasoned discussions of the sort we propose. On the other hand, Robert Wuthnow suggests,

> If one views the situation from the standpoint of Christian principles . . . one can only decry the ill will, the absence of brotherly and sisterly love, and the prevalence of dogmatism and bigotry that characterize present relations between conservative and liberal Christians. Scholars on both sides who care about the Christian virtues of harmony and reconciliation could clearly take a more active role in understanding and helping to mitigate these conflicts.[10]

Although tensions are great and the task of reconciliation is difficult, tensions regarding homosexuality must be kept in context and not exaggerated. The archbishop of Canterbury, George Carey, has noted that "our society has more problems with heterosexuality than homosexuality. . . . In my experience as a bishop, I have had more to do in wrestling with these issues."[11]

Conflict, division, and separation are hardly foreign to the history of Christ's church. The Bible from beginning to end recounts stories of conflict and controversy, disagreement and divergence. From the congregations to whom Paul wrote, through the Protestant Reformation and into the present, the history of the church has been one of friction, dispute, schism, and sometimes even violence over what it means to be a faithful follower of Jesus Christ. Repeatedly, people calling themselves Christian have isolated themselves from one another, often in self-righteous ways, each group claiming to know the absolute truth.

In the eyes of God, surely such behavior constitutes sin. When we call each other names, fail to listen to each other carefully, and become smug in our own positions, the Christ we seek to serve is betrayed. In our human frailty, are we doomed to misbehave in this way, or can we do better?

Claiming Our Common Ground

This book attempts to offer a framework by which Christians with widely diverse convictions can disagree in love while debating with integrity. For those who are neither gay nor lesbian, the disagreement and dialogue benefit from what has been called the "heterosexist privilege." It is not their own humanity or inclusion within the Body of Christ that is being debated. Thus, the danger exists of depersonalizing homosexuality and failing to hear the voices of the persons being hurt and excluded to facilitate a false harmony within the church. We hope the format of this book does not tolerate the diminishing of anyone's personhood; rather, it encourages deeper understanding of the complexities of human sexuality and theology. While the editors have their own views on this subject, it is their intent not to be advocates in this book of a particular position but to provide an opportunity for meaningful dialogue. If it helps members of even one family or congregation to be more informed and/or more understanding, the editors will be satisfied.

Therefore, it is imperative to underscore the principles that mainline Christian denominations profess as fundamental to their faith.[12] Within the following chapters, these ten axioms will serve as precepts for all those who have written essays. Thus, certain positions, which might take quite extreme stances on the political and religious right or left, are not included in this volume. Though this book encourages tolerance of differing ideas, even openness has some limits, since inaccurate information, deliberate lies, and outright hatred have no justifiable place in legitimate scholarship or church dialogue. Within these general parameters, conscientious Christian writers—homosexual and heterosexual—discuss various understandings and differences of opinion about the inclusion and/or exclusion of homosexual persons within the church.

First, we assert Scripture to be the primary source of understanding about the meaning and will of God, and we acknowledge that in our attempts to grasp its meaning we need to use reason, tradition, and experience. Contrasting differences of opinion regarding homosexuality often develop because we understand and use the Bible differently.

Second, we affirm the Great Commandment of Jesus to love your neighbor as yourself. This injunction means different things to different Christians, but all of us strive to live by it. There are sharp disparities in Christian interpretations of what it means to love persons whose sexual orientation and/or practice is homosexual.

Third, we believe in human dignity, believing each person is a child of God created in God's image. We differ in our understandings about the role of homosexual persons as participants in the fellowship of the church, but we agree that every person is of sacred worth.

Fourth, we advocate pastoral care for all persons. The ministry and love of the church are meant for all persons in their search for meaning and fulfillment. No person shall be denied the sacraments and other gifts of care that the church offers.

Fifth, we call for the protection of human rights and civil liberties for all persons. Legal discrimination in jobs, housing, or other areas is wrong, and we work to eliminate discrimination. Differences of opinion occur when some interpret protective legislation for lesbians and gays as the creation of special rights.

Sixth, we accept the reality of human sin. Christians understand that each person is in need of grace. None of us is capable of living a life in perfect harmony with God, just as none of us can accurately judge the sinfulness of others. Whether homosexuality is a sin, and if so, how serious a sin, is a matter of theological contention.

Seventh, we recognize that sexuality is God's good gift for all persons. Sexuality is a fundamental part of human identity. It is one expression of our need for companionship and for intimate sharing. Sexuality is also at the foundation of family structure and the creation and nurture of children. Where Christians differ is whether homosexual expressions of love can be affirmed.

Eighth, we maintain there must be boundaries and restrictions on certain human behavior, including sexual misconduct. Christians oppose sexual exploitation and violence directed to any person.

The abuse of women and children is especially deplorable. Defining these boundaries sometimes becomes problematic. Christians diverge in their opinions as to whether homosexual activity between consenting adults constitutes sexual misconduct or an expression of God's good gift.

Ninth, we profess the church as the community of the faithful and seek to preserve and strengthen it. Sexual orientation should be no barrier to membership. What divides Christians is whether homosexual practice should disqualify gay and lesbian persons from being full participants in the mission and ministry of the church.

Tenth, we acknowledge that no person fully understands the will of God. Each of us knows that he or she sees through the divine glass darkly. Each of us lives with the knowledge that no matter how firmly we hold a conviction, we are in danger of being wrong. We approach this inquiry with humility.

Topics That Trouble the Church

As the editors are rooted in the Wesleyan tradition, perhaps it is not surprising that John Wesley's quadrilateral became the framework within which the book was constructed. The four sources of theology—Scripture, tradition, experience, and reason—are woven through each chapter of the book as recurring threads or themes. The topics through which they wind are those the editors deem most contentious within local congregations as well as within denomination policy decision-making bodies. They include biblical interpretation, the compatibility of homosexuality with Christianity, interpretation of scientific data about the causes and meaning of homosexuality, appropriate ways to offer pastoral care to persons of same-sex orientation and their families, ordination of lesbians and gays, and legitimation of same-sex unions.

Following the two papers written by authors of divergent points of view, a third section, written by the editors, enumerates the major themes of the chapter and offers a list of questions that may be used to stimulate group discussion. Some readers may find it helpful to read in reverse, looking at this editorial section of each chapter before reading the two position papers.

The questions are followed by a short list of resources for those who wish further study. Most are accessible in public libraries; all are appropriate for local church pastors and laity. Those who wish to do in-depth study are encouraged to consult their nearest seminary or denominational office for suggestions. A periodic review of *Sojourners, Christianity Today, The Christian Century,* and *The Other Side* may result in the discovery of helpful new materials. These four periodicals, representing both conservative and liberal perspectives, frequently deal with controversial subjects of concern to persons in the religious community.

Each editor has contributed a chapter. Sally B. Geis, using the descriptive methodology of a sociologist who has worked extensively with homosexual persons, offers a chapter of stories about gays and lesbians, their families, and their church-related experiences. The reader is asked to consider what role the church can or should play in the lives of the persons involved.

In the concluding chapter, Donald E. Messer draws on his background as pastor, Christian ethicist, and seminary president, as he invites readers to weave their own theologies of homosexuality.

Some Editorial Clarifications

Certain editorial policies and perspectives inform the content and structure of this book.

1. The book was developed and designed for ecumenical use. The writers come from many denominations: Roman Catholic, Presbyterian Church U.S.A., United Church of Christ, American Baptist, Evangelical Lutheran Church of America, and The United Methodist Church.

2. A number of important topics related to the general subject of homosexuality are omitted from this book. Bisexuality, AIDS, lesbian or gay parenting, military

service, and a host of other topics are not addressed in detail. Limitations of time and space required selectivity.

3. The editors have sought to be objective and even-handed in the treatment of the subject, but they are not neutral. Both editors believe the church should be fully accepting of all persons, including those of same-sex orientation. They also believe it is imperative for persons who disagree to sustain ongoing conversation within local churches and denominational bodies rather than splinter into think-alike congregations or noncommunicating subgroups within denominations. Single-cause lobbying groups or causes within denominations can serve a useful purpose by highlighting the needs of powerless groups, but they also can become divisive forces doing more harm than good.

Disagreeing in Love

The following chapters illustrate dramatic difference in the way Christians think theologically about homosexuality. Their polarized essays on key questions facing the church and contemporary culture reflect the raging debate that is tearing apart many congregations and splitting families of faith. The primary division between Christians is no longer between Catholic and Protestant but between evangelicals and liberals. Too often, Robert Wuthnow reports, "Liberals look across the theological fence at their conservative cousins and see rigid, narrow-minded, moralistic fanatics; while conservatives holler back with taunts that liberals are immoral, loose, biblically illiterate, and unsaved."[13]

This book is based on the premise that all Christians, lay and clergy, should be encouraged to draw on their informed understanding of the Christian faith in making decisions regarding personal and social issues. We invite persons to reflect on human sexuality, both homosexuality and heterosexuality, in light of their best understanding of Christian faith and ethics, and to respond appropriately. Such individual reflection presumes not that all conscientious Christians of goodwill will reach the same conclusion but that persons will gain new insight, own their decisions, understand the implications, and be able to articulate intelligibly the Christian rationale for their stance.[14]

M. Kent Millard has described a model of thinking theologically about homosexuality that includes at least three steps: (1) seek accurate factual knowledge, (2) understand theological considerations, and (3) help persons make informed decisions.[15] At a minimum, Christians insist on the scientific facts as best they can be discerned, in accord with the Gospel of John's admonition to "know the truth" (John 8:32).[16] Likewise, considering theological information and implications is imperative for Christians, lest attitudes, opinions, and judgments be made without benefit of the church's historic/contemporary insights and scriptural/theological interpretations. To think theologically demands that we Christians decide now where we stand and how we respond, ever sensitive to God's guidance and ever open to God's grace. May our prayer be:

Lord,
Weave our lives together in love.
Make us a patchwork of kindred souls.
Let the patterns of our lives come together as one.
Stitch together the brokenness and remnants
    of our past to create a new design
    for living. Amen.[17]

NOTES

1. Robert Nugent, STM, and Jeannine Gramick, Ph.D., "Homosexuality: Protestant, Catholic and Jewish Issues: A Fishbone Tale," in *Homosexuality and Religion,* ed. Richard Hasbany (London & New York: Haworth Press, 1989), p. 7.

2. James Davison Hunter, quoted in "Divided We Stand," *Chicago Tribune,* Oct. 28, 1992, section 2, p. 2. See also James Davison Hunter, *Cultural Wars: The Struggle to Define America* (New York: Basic Books, 1991).

3. Ibid.

4. Kenneth Cracknell, *Towards a New Relationship: Christians and People of Other Faiths* (London: Epworth Press, 1986), pp. 110-27.

5. For a fuller explanation of these steps, see Donald E. Messer, *A Conspiracy of Goodness: Contemporary Images of Christian Mission* (Nashville: Abingdon Press, 1992), pp. 140-41.

6. Mary Wilcox, "Reflections and Implications: Six Months of Exploring the Issue of the Ordination of Gays/Lesbians/Bisexuals," May 1993. Unpublished paper used with permission.

7. Robert Wuthnow, *The Struggle for America's Soul* (Grand Rapids: Wm. B. Eerdmans Publishing Co., 1989), p. 185.

8. T. M. Scanlon, review of *Life's Dominion: An Argument about Abortion, Euthanasia, and Individual Freedom,* by Ronald Dworkin (New York: Knopf, 1993), *New York Review,* July 15, 1993, p. 50.

9. *U.S. News and World Report,* July 15, 1993, pp. 42-48.

10. Wuthnow, *The Struggle for America's Soul,* p. 185.

11. George Carey, archbishop of Canterbury, quoted in *The United Methodist Reporter,* Oct. 9, 1992, p. 2.

12. These ten statements are in accord with the "Social Principles" and "Our Theological Task" of The United Methodist Church. See *The Book of Discipline of The United Methodist Church, 1992,* par. 68, section 4, pp. 76-82, and par. 71, pp. 90-92. Similar declarations, with some variation, can be found in most other mainline Protestant denominational documents.

13. Robert Wuthnow, *The Restructuring of American Religion: Society and Faith Since World War II* (Princeton: Princeton University Press, 1988), p. 215.

14. See Robert A. Evans and Thomas D. Parker, eds., and others, *Christian Theology: A Case Study Approach* (New York: Harper & Row, 1976), p. 4.

15. See M. Kent Millard, "A Model for Enabling Christians to Think Theologically about Social Issues," D.Min. Project, McCormick Theological Seminary, 1979. One of the coeditors of this book, Donald E. Messer, was the project supervisor.

16. C. H. Dodd, in *Interpretation of the Fourth Gospel* (Cambridge: Cambridge University Press, 1963), pp. 176-77, demonstrates that "truth" as used in John's Gospel refers both to knowledge of divine reality and to statements simply corresponding to the facts of a given matter. In John 4:18 and 10:41, truth refers to the simple idea that a statement corresponds to the actual facts.

17. T. Todd Masman, "Woven Together in Love," in *Meditations for HIV and AIDS Ministries,* eds. Patricia D. Brown and T. Todd Masman (New York: General Board of Global Ministries, 1993), p. 3.

STUDY GUIDE

This book seeks to provide some sign language so that persons with differing viewpoints can begin the process of reflective listening to one another, discerning points of agreement as well as learning to disagree in love. Ten principles of faith, common to many Christians, are stated and become the framework within which authors with contrasting positions are presented side by side to encourage informed study and debate. Each Christian is invited to reflect on sexuality, both heterosexuality and homosexuality, in light of his or her best understanding of Christian faith and ethics. Since sexual issues intersect at the crossroads of vital questions of human life and church teachings, persons cannot avoid personal decision making. This is not just a lonely debate within oneself; it is a living dialogue with one's neighbors.

Items for Reflection

1. Do you know anyone who is of same-sex orientation? In what setting—at work or church? Share experiences of meeting and knowing gay and lesbian persons.

2. This book presents contrasting opinions on homosexuality and the church. It may not be possible to read it without getting angry. How do we help people deal with their anger?

3. Can you and your study group agree to abide by some basic guidelines so that your debate can be fair and loving?

4. When you hear that someone is homosexual, how does it make you feel? Possible activity: write the words that come to your mind when you hear the term *homosexual*.

5. Would you be willing to have a gay or lesbian person speak to your study group? Do you think that balance would require having an ex-gay or ex-lesbian also share? If you couldn't get representatives of both sides, would you be upset to have only one side make a presentation?

SUGGESTED RESOURCES

Cohen, Daniel, and Susan Cohen. *When Someone You Know Is Gay.* New York: M. Evans & Co., 1989. Used by Federation of Parents and Friends of Lesbians and Gays, P. O. Box 27605, Washington, D.C. 20038-7605, an organization that supports acceptance of homosexual identity.

Lanning, Cynthia, ed. *Answers to Your Questions About Homosexuality.* Lexington, Ky.: Bristol Books, 1988. Used by a number of ex-gay organizations that believe homosexuals should and can be changed to heterosexuals.

"The Loving Opposition, Our Response to the Homosexual Crisis." *Christianity Today,* July 19, 1993. Includes editorials and articles by evangelical writers.

Toward a Christian Understanding of Sexual Orientations, Lifestyles and Ministry. Recommendations and Report to the 32nd General Council from the Division of Ministry Personnel and Education and the Division of Mission in Canada, Feb. 19, 1988.

"What the Church Can and Cannot Responsibly Teach about Homosexuality," from *The Report by the United Methodist Committee to Study Homosexuality,* 1992. See Appendix A of this book.

CHAPTER 1

THE HUMAN FACES OF HOMOSEXUALITY

Sally B. Geis

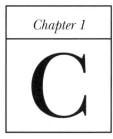

Chapter 1

Church discussions about homosexuality often include references to *the* homosexual life-style as if a single pattern of behavior describes the lives of all gay and lesbian persons. In fact, no one story accurately describes the sexual relationships and fantasies of any category of human beings, including gay and lesbian persons. Sexuality is an intimate, deeply personal part of each person's identity, too complex and too interconnected with other behavior patterns and values to be reduced to a single description. Therefore, it is no more possible to identify *the* homosexual life-style than to identify *the* heterosexual life-style.

When the role of gays and lesbians becomes a topic for debate within the church, we need to remember we are talking about people rather than about an abstract concept. Remarks about who "they" are and what "they" should do need to be tempered with a genuine understanding of human experience. Understandings about the life-styles of homosexual persons come from personal encounters with individuals of same-sex orientation.

Homosexual Stereotypes

Assumptions about the existence of *the* homosexual life-style develop as all stereotypes develop, from a fear of persons who are "different" from the majority, from a fear of strangers. Christians are called to remember how Jesus treated strangers and to resist all stereotyping, including the stereotyping of homosexual persons.

However, since stereotypes of homosexual persons are so common, it is important to refute some of the most persistent ones. The characteristics discussed below undoubtedly describe some homosexual persons as well as some heterosexual ones. The unfairness of stereotyping is the assumption that these negative descriptions fit all or even most persons who are gay or lesbian.

Myths About Homosexual People

1. *They are child molesters.* This myth is false. There is no evidence that the propensity to molest children is a characteristic linked to sexual orientation. Only 2.5 percent of the juvenile offenders seen by the Kempe National Center for Prevention and Treatment of Child Abuse are identified as homosexual.[1] Most child molestation occurs in interfamily situations, predominantly heterosexual families. The one characteristic statistically linked to child molestation is alcoholism. Social scientists attribute society's emphasis on homosexual molestation to the cultural stigma that surrounds *all* homosexual behavior. Heterosexual abuse apparently seems more "normal."

2. *They are unhappy, maladjusted people.* The problems with defining and measuring happiness in any population are enormous, so scholars seldom try. Although Ann Landers hardly qualifies as a scientific source, it is interesting to note the responses she received to her inquiry: "Are you glad you're gay, or would you rather be straight?" She quit counting after 75,875 responses, but she reported that 30 to 1 persons said they were glad they were gay and did not wish to be different.[2]

Maladjustment is also difficult to measure, but there is abundant evidence that many highly successful persons are of same-sex orientation. When an acclaimed artist like Michelangelo, a successful attorney, or a trusted pastor is "discovered" to be gay or lesbian, it usually comes as a shock to colleagues and friends who are straight because the person "seems so normal."

3. *They are promiscuous.* The initial problem with measurements of promiscuity is one of definition. *Webster's Ninth New Collegiate Dictionary* defines *promiscuity* as "a miscellaneous mixture or mingling of persons or things." The definition says nothing about how many persons or things need to be mixed or how to create promiscuity. Are we to count every man and every woman, heterosexual or homosexual, who has more than one sex partner in a lifetime? more than one sex partner at any given moment in time? A heterosexual person who divorces and remarries is not considered promiscuous unless the person divorces and marries frequently. Since homosexual unions are not a legitimate option in the eyes of the church, are we to count all gay and lesbian persons who have serial, monogamous sexual relationships as promiscuous? How many partners are required and under what circumstances to create a promiscuous situation? These are not frivolous questions. Without accurate definition no objective conclusions can be drawn.

The second problem with promiscuity measurement involves accurate data collection. It is always difficult to collect objective data by asking subjective questions. It is particularly difficult to assess the validity of promiscuity data because some people, regardless of sexual orientation, wish to hide their sexual indiscretions. A job, a marriage, or a reputation may be at stake if one is "found out." On the other hand, others wishing to appear "macho" tend to exaggerate their sexual conquests! There is no good way for social scientists to guarantee either the validity or the reliability of promiscuity data, though there does seem to be consistent evidence that men treat sex more casually than women and are apt to have more partners.

Opponents in ideological debates about homosexuality frequently use descriptive data to prove a point without considering the accuracy of the source. Such usage leads many people to believe, "You can make numbers say whatever you want them to say!"

In the case of homosexuality, the misuse of Alfred Kinsey's work is a classic example. From a social scientist's point of view, his work was a major breakthrough in content and methodology. Never before had an attempt been made to collect data on sexual behavior from a large sample of people. Much was learned about the complexity of measurement, the validity and reliability of results.

Unfortunately, persons with ideological intent began using his numbers to bolster arguments about the rightness or wrongness of behavior. Liberals used his estimate of 10 percent as the percentage of homosexual persons in the total population to "prove" that homosexuality was normal. Conservatives ignored those numbers until new studies suggested lower percentages. Now conservatives use lower numbers to suggest homosexuality must not be normal after all if only 3 or 2 or 1 percent of the population is same-sex oriented. Each side quotes numbers as if (1) any number could be absolutely valid and reliable, particularly in a social climate as politically charged as contemporary America's; (2) numbers are relevant to one's moral and ethical conclusions about behavior.

Promiscuity number counting presents all the same problems. Conservatives frequently quote a 1970 study by Allen P. Bell and Martin S. Weinberg that suggested high rates of promiscuity among gay men. More recent studies, particularly since the advent of AIDS, quote entirely different numbers. Liberals like these studies better.

Almost daily, newspapers report on the frequency of sexual activity in one group or another. To the embarrassment of the church in all its branches, Catholic and Protestant, conservative and liberal, reports of sexual misconduct, most of it heterosexual, abound. It hardly seems relevant to label the homosexual segment of the population as promiscuous when most segments seem to have a high percentage of persons who are neither celibate nor faithful partners in monogamous marriages.

4. *They are aggressive and enjoy forcing their life-style onto others who find it distasteful.* A high-visibility segment of urban gay culture feeds this assumption that an aggressive, flamboyant subculture represents all gay and lesbian persons. Most people with same-sex orientation belong to the large closeted, or invisible, population of homosexual persons. Most of them expend great effort

hiding their orientation rather than flaunting it. It is no more accurate to assume all homosexual persons are members of highly visible groups such as Act Up or Queer Nation than to assume all teenagers are hard rock music devotees. These subcultures do exist, but they do not represent the vast majority of persons within either group.

Many gay and lesbian persons live as couples, just as heterosexual persons do. As Philip Blumstein and Pepper Schwartz discovered in their massive study *American Couples,* gay and lesbian people go to work and come home to wash the car or take out the garbage like everybody else.

This study, considered by many to be the most comprehensive study of American couples done to date, involved twelve thousand couples over an eighteen-month period. Its purpose was to assess the effects of recent radical changes in family structure on the lives of different kinds of couples. It focused primarily on discovering "why they [the couples] make the choices they do, and if those choices prove gratifying."[3]

Since society's broadening definition of acceptable living arrangements includes increasing numbers of unmarried heterosexual couples, they were included in the study along with married couples. Gay and lesbian couples were also included because so little research has been done on them. "Almost all the competent, non-moralistic research on homosexuality" has been conducted since 1970, and most of that research involved single gay men rather than lesbians or homosexual couples.[4] This omission from research literature prevails in spite of research findings that indicate " 'couplehood,' either as a reality or an aspiration, is as strong among gay people as it is among heterosexuals."[5]

The results suggest there is less difference among different kinds of couples than one might expect. Furthermore, whether one is male or female is a more important factor in defining one's attitudes toward couple behavior than is sexual orientation.

Stories About Homosexuality in Church Families

An issue closely related to stereotyping is the tendency to think of gay and lesbian persons, even couples, as separate from the rest of society. This, too, is false. They do not live in isolation. They have parents, spouses, lovers, friends, and coworkers, just as heterosexual people do. Many families with gay or lesbian members are as closeted or in some cases more closeted than the individual member of same-sex orientation. They remain silent, fearful that there is no safe place to share their stories. When homosexuality is discussed within the church, all of the involved persons need to be considered.

The true stories of church families told here have been altered to protect individual identity. Some readers will find themselves in the stories; others will be surprised that these are the stories of persons who belong to local churches across America. Selecting a few stories to illustrate a larger, more varied group of stories is hazardous. Some readers may feel these are not the most representative assortment. Others may regret omissions. Our criteria for choice are threefold:

1. The stories illustrate the complexity of human experience and are not intended to prove the correctness of either a liberal or conservative interpretation. The reader is encouraged to apply his or her theology to an understanding of the stories.
2. The ultimate focus of each story is on the role of the church since the purpose of this book is to consider the church's ministry with homosexual persons.
3. The stories are meant to be as inclusive as possible, free from ageism, sexism, or racism.

A Hopeful Stance

Many of the stories about homosexuality and the church are filled with pain. Lest we become too discouraged, listen to these voices. Though these two persons understand the relationship between their homosexuality and their Christian faith in totally different ways, both persons live within the church with a qualified measure of hope. The ex-gay man still has homosexual feelings and works daily to keep them under control. It is a painful, difficult task. The lesbian woman has found a local church that accepts her, but the denomination to which she belongs still maintains an official stance saying homosexuality is incompatible with Christian teaching.

An Ex-Gay Evangelical Man

> I was a homosexual, but I don't believe God made me that way. The church did not have to say it was wrong, I knew it inside. When I met Jesus I knew I could change. I never had feelings other than homosexual until I became a Christian. That was ten years ago. I continue to try to become more Christ like each day. Ten years ago God gave me a wife and three children. I am living by grace day after day. My church accepts me, holds me accountable. People are there for me.[6]

A Mainline, Liberal Lesbian

> In the book *All I Really Need to Know I Learned in Kindergarten*, Unitarian minister Robert Fulghum tells about a game in which children were asked to decide whether they wanted to be Giants, Wizards, or Dwarfs. After a child decided on a category, she or he was to go to the place designated for that group. But one little girl kept asking, "Where do the mermaids stand?" She refused to pretend to be somebody else; she knew her category. The minister who was king of the game realized that she had faith that there *was* a place for mermaids and that she was not going to hang her head and not play. Finally, he was won over by her honesty and said, "Mermaids stand here beside the king." As a lesbian, I have always felt that Christ has said to me, "Stand here beside the King."[7]

A Grandparent Story

The husband in this couple is a deacon in his church; his wife is a past president of the women's society. One Christmas the pair made their usual trip to a large southern city to spend the holidays with their son, daughter-in-law, and three young grandchildren. The grandparents arrived with the traditional homemade cookies, the family Bible from which the grandfather reads the Christmas story to the children each Christmas Eve, and presents for all. On their arrival they discovered that their daughter-in-law left home the previous week with her lesbian lover.

What were they to do? They did what many grandparents would do. They thought less about themselves than about their devastated son and their confused grandchildren. They tried to make Christmas as normal as possible. Grandmother cooked the turkey. Grandfather put the new dollhouse together. Everyone sang "Silent Night" before the children were put to bed on Christmas Eve.

But after the tree came down and the presents were put away, the grandparents turned to prayer as Christians do in times of suffering and bewilderment. They prayed for guidance: "What would Jesus have us do now?" They concluded there was no choice but to reach out to the woman who was the mother of their grandchildren and try to understand her actions.

Within a few months the daughter-in-law's parents disowned her, and they withdrew into virtual seclusion. The young woman's mother suffers from deep depression and blames herself for this terrible tragedy. "What did I do wrong?" she asks.

Their son is still angry with the wife from whom he is now divorced, but time seems to be healing his wounds. He has begun dating a woman with whom he works; perhaps he will marry again. In retrospect he is able to say the marriage was never very satisfying, something was always missing but he did not know what it was.

The grandchildren are going through all the emotional stress that divorce brings, but they, too, are adjusting. They live with their father and visit their mother once a month for the weekend.

The rationale the grandparents offer for their nonjudgmental stance toward their former daughter-in-law is that God's greatest commandment is for us to show love and compassion to all.

They will leave judgment about her action to God. They are particularly concerned about maintaining a family atmosphere in which their grandchildren can be open to their mother's love.

On the other hand, they are relieved that their son has custody of the children, partly because they believe the Bible says homosexuality is a sin. How serious a sin they do not know, but they would rather the mother not raise the children in a lesbian family.

The lesbian mother grieves the loss of her children in the divorce settlement and looks forward to their monthly visits. She wishes she could help her parents understand the life to which she was conforming as a straight, married woman was a hollow existence filled with pretense and fear. She simply could not go on with the charade any longer.

What is the church's role in this family's struggle? The grandparents still attend their local church but not as regularly. They feel less at home in the congregation than before the breakup of their son's marriage. When they shared their plan with a few members of the congregation, they were met with mixed reactions. Some persons affirmed their efforts to accept their daughter-in-law, but many did not. Going to church is not as comforting as it once was.

The son occasionally takes his children to church school because he wants them to have some instruction in Christian values, but he feels out of place in the congregation and drops the children off without attending worship himself. The daughter-in-law attends a Metropolitan Community Church because she feels more welcome there than in a mainline church.

One Gay Man's Lover

Raised in a small town in Ohio, a young man and his family were involved in church activities. He even considered the ministry as a calling. One factor influencing his decision to become a nurse instead was his sexual orientation. He knew he was "different" from the time he was a young boy. He also knew what the junior high school health class teacher said when he took all the boys to a separate room for one of his talks, "Watch out for homos. They're the lowest, most perverted, sick, sadistic people in the world." He also knew how his church felt. There he learned they are an abomination in God's sight and worthy of death. Finally, the burden of rejection by "respectable" society became so great that he tried to heal his wounds by saying he no longer cared what anybody, especially people in the church, thought of him.

As part of his rebellion against his past, he moved to San Francisco and started doing things that would shock his family. He frequented gay bars and bathhouses. He joined a gay pride parade. When his parents learned he was living in San Francisco, his mother came to plead with him to renounce the new life and refrain from associating with homosexual persons.

When she asked how he could do such a thing, knowing how much it hurt her and his father, he was unable to make her understand. All he could say was that he could no longer live in a "cage of pretense." Being with the new friends who shared his need for acceptance made him feel like a *real* person. He had freedom and a sense of personal dignity he never experienced before. He could not give up those feelings.

During his time in San Francisco, he met and fell in love with another young man much like himself. His lover's background was much like his own except that the other young man's parents were not even willing to talk about sexual orientation. When they learned their son was gay, they told him never to communicate with them again. They treated him as if he were dead.

In time the two young men wearied of the life they were leading and realized it had served its purpose. They had discovered each other and developed some self-esteem. They felt so good about themselves as human beings they no longer needed to live in a gay ghetto for support.

Together they left San Francisco, moved to a small Midwestern town, and joined a mainline church that would accept them as a couple. They wished they could make a religious public commitment of their loyalty to each other, but church law did not permit it. The young man renewed his nursing license and began working in the cancer ward of a hospital where he continues working to this day. His partner found work as a graphic artist. Together they bought a home and became productive members of the community.

After about two years of the new life, the nurse's partner began losing weight and experiencing frequent bouts with viral infections. Eventually, he was diagnosed with HIV infection. For another year or more they made the best of it, coping with intermittent episodes of illness. Gradually, illness became a way of life, and the nurse devoted most of his time to the care of his dying partner. They fought all the usual battles—apartment house evictions when the cause of illness was discovered, ambulance drivers who would not respond to calls, hospital attendants who would not enter the room.

As the patient's condition deteriorated, the nurse decided to try contacting the patient's parents. He hoped their son's impending death would move them to reconciliation. The parents refused to come unless their son was willing to repent and accept the fact that his death was a punishment for the sinful life he had led.

With some trepidation the nurse urged them to come and at least talk with their son. He knew he was taking a calculated risk. The visit could be a disaster, but he knew how much his lover wanted to see his parents one more time and say good-bye. Furthermore, he prayed that the sight of their dying child would make the parents more gentle. The parents eventually came, but their attitude remained unchanged.

They visited twice during the last few months of their son's illness, each time urging him to repent. With what little energy the son had left, he tried to make his parents understand that he *was* sorry for the promiscuous and exploitive life he had led those few years in San Francisco. However, he could not reject the lover with whom he had shared so much joy, the partner who was caring for him so faithfully in sickness as well as in health—even to death.

Where was the church in these lives? The pastor and congregation of the couple's church were supportive through the illness and still support the nurse, who is now diagnosed as HIV positive. They do not believe that homosexuality is a sin. They also do not believe in a God who punishes with illness and death. They are angry with the patient's family because they interpret the parents' action as a needless effort to heap guilt and shame on a dying man.

The patient's parents are angry, too. They believe the permissive attitude of some churches is a major factor in their son's decision to enter the gay life-style. They feel churches that affirm gay life-styles should accept major responsibility for the deaths of young men like their son, who they believe is condemned to hell forever.

Since their son would not repent and asked to be buried from a church that supported his life-style, the parents felt they could not, in good conscience, attend the service. They bore their grief alone. The father, who has always been a very private man, continues to hold his grief inside him, saying almost nothing, even to his wife. Shortly after the funeral, he had a heart attack. Sometimes his wife thinks he is dying of a broken heart.

The Congregation and Its Pastor

The pastor was raised in a small conservative town in New England. From the time she was a little girl, she knew she was called to ministry. During her college and seminary days, she dated as girls were supposed to do, but always wondered why dating never excited her the way it seemed to excite other girls. Of course she expected to marry. In her denomination it would be difficult to find a congregation to accept any female pastor. Finding a congregation willing to accept a single pastor was almost unthinkable!

Shortly before graduation, she married another divinity student. They had much in common. He shared her interest in music, and both were committed to local church ministry. After their marriage, both received appointments as associates in churches in a large metropolitan area. Her appointment was in a high steeple church serving primarily young to middle-aged professionals.

To her dismay, she developed a deep sexual attraction toward a member of the congregation, a single attorney. Although she had experienced sexual fantasies about women since she was a young girl, none had been so strong. The two women worked together on a highly successful program for homeless teenagers. One evening the two were overcome by passion and acted on their sexual feelings.

Frightened by her emotions, terrified that she would be found out, the young woman began suffering from bouts of depression. Unable to tell anyone of her anguish, she decided pregnancy and the birth of a child would help her feel more "normal." In time she gave birth to a baby girl whom she loves deeply. She also asked to be moved from her appointment in the church where her lover belongs.

A dozen years have gone by. She and her husband subsequently became the parents of a bright and active little boy. The denominational officials and the local church parishioners see the family as an example of the perfect Christian family.

She is now the sole pastor in a church of her own. Her husband is an associate in a very large church nearby. She has never been able to bring herself to tell her husband her secret, but he realizes she is becoming more and more withdrawn. He has urged her to see a therapist for her depression, but she resists going for fear of being found out. He has suggested they see a marriage counselor together.

Recently, she asked him to sleep in a separate bedroom, at least for a while. He wonders how long this will go on, and he worries about his ability to stay faithful and celibate during this ordeal. He asks himself, How long can I live this way?

She wrote the following anonymous letter to the pastor of a large church in another denomination who is known as an outspoken advocate of gay and lesbian rights:

> I think I should call this a letter from prison, because that is what it is. I suppose I have "known" I was homosexual for a long time but I put the word in quotation marks because of the combination of ambivalence, uncertainty, and denial.

Even as I write I feel ill at ease because I have never before written "I am a homosexual." I do not want to be what I apparently am. Who in their right mind would willingly choose to be a homosexual in this society? What I am, as people around me see me, is a 37 year old married woman with two beautiful children, but I am miserable. I no longer seem to be able to connect in any way: spiritually, sexually or socially. Some people have a "neurotic" fear that if they let others know them, they would be rejected. For homosexuals, it is not a neurotic fear, it is reality. The strain of being in the pulpit each Sunday talking about wholeness, hope and love is destroying me.

Where is the church in this story? Ironically, the church seems virtually absent in the *life* of this family, which is so deeply enmeshed in the *structure* of the church. Psychiatry tells us that "unthinkable thoughts" are the thoughts that drive persons into the most painful and dangerous mental states. Deep and shameful secrets, despair, and feelings of hopelessness are sometimes the motivation for suicide.

Interpreting These Stories

Each reader will form his or her opinions and judgments about these stories and the people involved in them. Formulating "correct" Christian outcomes is not my reason for telling them. My purpose is to underscore the complexity and pain of living with homosexuality in our churches.

Kenneth J. Doka's recent book, *Disenfranchised Grief,* focuses on the needs of persons who have experienced losses that are not recognized or validated by others. The death of an ex-spouse, the miscarriage of a wanted child, or even the death of a pet may fall into this category, and so does the grief of the persons in the situations described above. According to Doka,

Disenfranchisement can occur when a society inhibits grief by establishing "grieving norms" that deny such emotions to persons deemed to have insignificant losses, insignificant relationship, or an insignificant capacity to grieve. . . . The be-reaved may experience a deep sense of shame about the relationship or they may experience emotions, perhaps re-flecting societal norms, that inhibit the grieving process.[8]

Doka goes on to point out that the intersocial and intrapsychic results are detrimental to persons, families, and communities.

Earlier in this chapter, I suggested there is no compelling evidence to suggest persons of same-sex orientation are any more maladjusted or unhappy than heterosexual persons. Yet most of the stories written or told about homosexual persons in the church are filled with pain. Not only has the church failed to stand with these persons in comfort and support, it has played a role in their disenfranchisement! We who call ourselves Christians, liberals and conservatives alike, need to reexamine our theologies and ask ourselves how this can be.

Our Task

Colin Cook, founder of the evangelical organization Quest: Ministries to the Broken, has said, "If ever there was a *first* place a homosexual should be able to turn to for help, it is the church. In fact, it is often the last. Why does the church stand silent and embarrassed over an issue that has spread despair to untold thousands?"[9] Too often, the "silent" voices of disenfranchised persons within the Christian community go virtually unnoticed as we debate rules and policies related to homosexuality. Too often, we talk *about* homosexuality without even bothering to know whether any homosexual persons or members of their families are present. Let us never forget this issue has a human face.

NOTES

1. Gail Ryan, facilitator of the Perpetration Prevention Project, Kempe National Center for Prevention and Treatment of Child Abuse, University of Colorado Health Sciences Center, Denver, Colorado, telephone interview, July 1993.

2. Ann Landers, *Minneapolis Star Tribune*, April 29, 1992, p. 2E.

3. Philip Blumstein and Pepper Schwartz, *American Couples* (New York: Pocket Books, 1983).

4. Ibid., p. 39.

5. Letitia Anne Peplau, Christine Padesky, and Mykol Hamilton, "Satisfaction in Lesbian Relationships," *Journal of Homosexuality* 8 (Winter 1982): 23-26, as quoted in Blumstein and Schwartz, p. 45.

6. Robert L. Kuyper, ed., Transforming Congregations (newsletter), Bakersfield, California, Jan. 1991.

7. Based on comments by Norma L. Kearby, M.D., during her testimony before the United Methodist Committee to Study Homosexuality, St. Louis, Missouri: Jan. 31, 1991.

8. Kenneth J. Doka, *Disenfranchised Grief* (Lexington Books, 1989), p. xv. See also Section II. Disenfranchised Relationships, chapter 4, "Lovers and Significant Others," by Ruth L. Fuller, Sally B. Geis, and Julian Rush, pp. 33-42.

9. Colin Cook, cover statement on a pamphlet advertising a seminar, Something Has Gone Wrong, offered by Where Grace Abounds, Denver, Colorado, April 25-26, 1991.

STUDY GUIDE

Thinking theologically about homosexuality requires hearing and taking into account the experiences of Christian gays and lesbians. Stereotypes of homosexual persons are examined. Personal stories of persons, their families, and their church-related experiences are told, lest this book simply be an impersonal, theoretical debate about issues that in reality reflect great struggle, pain, courage, and hope. Space limitations prohibit describing in detail the diversity of human experiences.

Homosexual is an adjective, not a noun, describing a dimension of a person's life rather than totally defining a human being.

Items for Reflection

1. Do you think most persons in your local church know the stereotypes of homosexual persons discussed in this chapter are not true?

2. How important is it to Christian decision making about

homosexuality and the church to know the percentage of gays and lesbians in the population?

3. Could there be any persons living the stories of this chapter in your local church?

4. How would you feel if you were to learn that your son or daughter were gay or lesbian? What would you want for your child?

SUGGESTED RESOURCES

Blumstein, Philip, and Pepper Schwartz. *American Couples.* New York: Pocket Books, 1983. A survey of 12,000 couples including married couples, cohabiting heterosexual couples, gay couples, and lesbian couples. Includes interviews and statistical analysis of life-style issues, such as the use of money, work life, and sexual behavior.

Consiglio, William. *Homosexual No More.* Wheaton, Ill.: Scripture Press, 1991. Used by ex-gay organizations.

Greenberg, David F. *The Social Construction of Homosexuality.* Chicago: University of Chicago Press, 1988. Both conservatives and liberals cite parts of this classic historical study as affirmation of their positions.

Pennington, Sylvia. *Ex-Gays? There Are None.* Hawthorne, Calif.: Lambda Christian Fellowship, 1989. Used by Parents and Friends of Lesbians and Gays.

CHAPTER 2

WHAT DOES THE BIBLE SAY ABOUT HOMOSEXUALITY?

Richard Clark Kroeger & Catherine Clark Kroeger

e believe that the Bible is our ultimate source for understanding ethics, sexuality, and the plans and purposes of God. In the case of the early chapters of Genesis, the language is so simple that a child can easily understand. This is a great blessing, for answers come easily when profound questions are raised by the most inquiring of minds—those of two- and three-year-olds. In the first three chapters of Genesis, we are given a very basic framework by which to understand such questions as, How did the world begin? Who am I? Who made me? Why was I made? Why did God make people male or female? As we mature, our understanding develops; and we see that the simple Creation story is actually very profound and a basis for a great deal of our biblical faith. We need to perceive it not childishly but with childlike faith.

Although some people argue that the first two chapters of Genesis are contradictory, we maintain that they supplement each other. The first chapter tells us that both male and female elements were present at creation and shared equally in the image of God (Gen. 1:26-27). The second chapter is a more detailed account of the rationale for creating two sexes. Despite the goodness of all else, God declared man's aloneness "not good," and woman was a precious gift who completed him. In vain Adam reviewed all the animals in hope of a companion, but no soul mate could be found (Gen. 2:20).

When Adam finally received a "partner corresponding to him" (Hebrew *'ezer kenegdo*), he burst into song: "This at last is bone of my bones and flesh of my flesh." Here is someone with whom he may share his inmost being. As God is a relational triune deity, so Adam and Eve together as one flesh reflected the image of God.

Besides the specific commandments for the safeguarding of marriage (Exod. 20:14; Deut. 5:18; 22:13-30), the Hebrew Bible, especially Leviticus 18 and 20, details a number of behaviors as destructive. Among other sexual expressions described as defiling to the participants (Lev. 18:8, 20, 23, 24; 20:3), homosexuality—males lying with males—is listed twice (18:22; 20:13). Aside from two descriptions of thwarted attempts at homosexual gang rape (Gen. 19:1-11; Judg. 19:1-30) and references to male cult prostitutes, little more is said on the subject in the Old Testament.

Christ quoted Genesis 2:24 when he affirmed marriage, thereby diverting attention from the petty legalism of divorce to the constructive and positive union of man and woman as the original intention of the Creator. They are glued together to become one flesh (Matt. 19:5-6; Mark 6:17-18). In superseding the Law of Moses, Jesus' emphasis moves woman from the status of property to that of a fully equal person, sharing the commitment, responsibilities, and privileges of marriage. This mutuality of trust and commitment is broken by the destructive nature of *porneia*. *Porneia*, though usually translated "fornication," can imply any inappropriate, immoral, or indecent sexual conduct. This term, as we shall see, was a catchword that included homosexuality within it. Persons involved in *porneia* were *pornoi*, and they violated God's plan as set forth in Genesis 1–3.

Pornographic representations of homoerotic acts have been recovered from every major city in Palestine—including Jerusalem.[1] A substantial number date to the Roman period, and they attest that the society of Jesus' and Paul's day was not ignorant of homosexual practices in its midst. Unions between consenting adults, same-sex marriages, group sex, and casual liaisons are all attested in Greco-Roman literature. As an amazingly versatile citizen of the ancient world, Paul, apostle to the Gentiles, indicates considerable knowledge of the diverse sexual activities current in his day. The epicenter was Rome, but the shock waves traveled throughout the empire.

An Ancient Perplexity

A favorite topic of Greco-Roman conversation was the debate about whether homosexual or heterosexual love was to be preferred.[2] Euripides' *Andromeda,* produced in 412 B.C., was a tremendous sensation because it suggested that the love object of a man might actually be a woman rather than another man. A thinker of the late first century A.D. declares, "Genuine love has no connection whatsoever with the women's quarters. I deny that it is love that you have felt for women or girls."[3] Such discussions continued until well past the New Testament period and usually tilted in the direction of homoerotic expression. If newly converted Gentiles came to Christianity with ambivalence on the matter of sexual choices, it is scarcely to be wondered. The Jerusalem Council, in its effort to integrate Gentiles, lifted many obligations of Jewish ritual but forbade *porneia* (Acts 15:20, 29).

The sexual values of Judaism were taken over into the church, especially the value of sexual purity. When Paul speaks in 1 Corinthians 6:16 of being joined to a prostitute, he literally says, "He that is glued to a prostitute is one body." The apparently casual union has claimed more from each participant than they might have imagined. Paul goes on to point out that the one who is glued to the Lord is one spirit (1 Cor. 6:17). The text continues, "Flee *porneia.* Every sin which an individual does is outside the body, but the one who is promiscuous sins within his body" (1 Cor. 6:18). The implication is that one inflicts upon and within oneself a spiritual, psychological, or even physical injury. The injury also extends to one's partner and to the community.

Paul recognizes sex as power—a power that may do either good or evil (1 Cor. 7:4, 14). He begins the discussion, "Because of the *porneias* [plural], let each man have his own wife and each woman her own husband" (1 Cor. 7:2). The driving force of sexuality may burst forth in many inappropriate modes. It is better to marry than to burn, yet both marriage and celibacy are gifts (1 Cor. 7:7, 9). The Apostle is remarkable in giving permission not to wed, despite Jewish insistence on marriage and the oppressive taxation exacted by the Roman government on persons who chose to remain unmarried.

The Matter of Definitions

Far more often than we are led to believe, the Bible approaches sex in positive terms. For instance, "Marriage is honorable in all and the bed unsoiled. For God will judge fornicators [*pornoi*] and adulterers" (Heb. 13:4). Promiscuous heterosexual activity is pinpointed for disapproval much more frequently than homosexual activity. In 1 Corinthians 6:9, Paul details the types of heterosexual and homosexual conduct that are unacceptable in the Body of Christ: "Neither the sexually immoral [*pornoi*] nor idolaters nor adulterers neither passive [*malakoi*] nor active homosexual partners [*arsenoikoitai*]."

To understand what is being said, we need to know the meaning of the Greek vocabulary. The rendering of these terms in the various translations changes, as do many other turns of expression, because language itself changes; and translations seek to adapt to contemporary needs. Remember also that translators struggle with the problem of putting blunt sexual language into terms that will not be unduly offensive to the readers. The meaning in Greek is quite clear—how to express it acceptably in English is something else again.

The words appear often enough in other writings so that we can understand the meaning of these terms. *Pornoi*—if used collectively—designates prostitutes or immoral persons of either sex. The term could mean either the active or the passive partner in homosexual intercourse.[4] *Malakoi*—as soft, effeminate, or the penetrated partner in homosexual intercourse[5]—is well attested in ancient literature, while *arenkoitai* indicates those who lie with a man as with a woman.[6] The placing of the two terms (*malakoi* and *arsenkoitai*) side by side indicates an awareness of the active and passive roles that might be played in a homosexual union, whether permanent or transitory. *Pornoi* occurs in 1 Timothy 1:10 as part of a condemnation of unlawful behavior and stands immediately before the more specific *arsenokoitai,* again denoting homosexuality.

God's Creation and Humankind's Rebellion

The beginning premise of the book of Romans is that all persons, whether Jews or Gentiles, are sinners, and all are in need of a Savior. Paul turns first to the Gentiles, who have been given a knowledge of God's glory through creation; but instead they turned to the worship of earthly likenesses. Indeed, they "worshiped the creation more than the Creator" and came to reap the consequences of the decisions made by their own free will. Both men and women had forsaken God's original purpose. The ultimate creative act of God was in drawing forth woman from man and bestowing her as a precious gift to Adam. To turn away from this precious gift constituted a rejection of God's creative benefaction, a distortion of the divine plan. Once devalued, "their women exchanged the natural use for that which is against nature" (Rom. 16:2).

The phrase "against nature" is used to describe homosexuality not only by Hellenistic Jewish writers but also by Greeks such as Plato.[7] As Paul suggests, sexual misconduct was associated with pagan practice and belief. The priestesses at the festival of the Haloa coached women in homosexual arts "whispering the instruction in their ears as though it were something which could not be spoken,"[8] while Roman women engaged in sexual play among themselves at the festival of the Good Goddess.[9] Religiously dictated bestiality and intercourse with phallic images were sometimes employed in female cults,[10] but the reference in Romans 1:26 cannot be narrowly tied to fertility rights. More broadly, it speaks of the relinquishing of male partners for other sorts of sexual activity.

"Likewise," the text continues, "the men, leaving the natural use of the female burned in their desire toward one another, males with males, working that which is shameful and receiving within themselves that recompense which is due their error" (1:27). Some people maintain that AIDS is a divine judgment on homosexuality rather than a consequence of one's choices. Repeatedly, the text emphasizes that people are granted free will. God "gives us over" to our choices and their consequences (Rom. 1:24, 26, 28). Paul insists on the necessity not to "suppress the truth" (1:18) about what God has made known to humanity, and the passage goes on to speak of a great many other kinds of inappropriate behaviors and attitudes on the part of those who refused to recognize the claims of their Creator. The rebels, knowing full well the decree of condemnation, not only participated in such conduct but gave their approval to others involved (Rom. 1:32). As servants of God, we are called not to give our approbation to certain behaviors but—like God—to give love, justice, and respect along with permission for others to exercise their own free will. The obligation of a prophet is to speak the truth as she or he understands it, but the response lies with the hearers. It is up to the individual whether or not to heed warnings that have been given.

Sexual Energy Rechanneled as Spiritual Energy

In his universal condemnation of humanity, Paul includes persons engaged in homosexual activities along with those who are haughty, greedy, extortioners, slanderers, abusers, plotters of evil, and a host of others. The central message of Romans is that "each one of us has sinned and come short of the glory of God" (Rom. 3:23), that "the wages of sin is death, but the gift of God is eternal life through Jesus Christ our Lord" (Rom. 6:23). Every human being is called to repentance and personal faith in

Christ; and as redeemed sinners, we seek to walk in newness of life. Repeatedly, believers are called to "put off the old" and "put on the new." One practice that we are called to discard is a physical/genital expression of homosexuality.

There is no extended discussion of sexual orientation as such in the New Testament, but desires, lusts, and passions are frequently addressed. In Christ, there are new relationships and new ways of dealing with one's urges. The writer of Colossians is aware that mere prohibition is of no value in controlling physical passions (2:22-23). There is a need to rechannel sexual energies. Believers are called upon to put off as dead *porneia* impurity, illicit passion, evil lusts, and greed (3:5). These are to be transformed into new and spiritual qualities: "compassion, kindness, humility, gentleness, patience, forbearing one another and forgiving if anyone has a grudge against another. . . . Above all, clothe yourselves with love, which binds everything together in perfect harmony" (3:12-14).

Christian Attitudes

This call applies to heterosexual persons and homosexual persons, and we would do well to remember that Paul also said, "My friends, if anyone is detected in a transgression, you who have received the Spirit should restore such a one in a spirit of gentleness" (Gal. 6:1). He added a reminder that the person doing the reproving may be the one at fault the next time.

Recently, we swam 1.4 miles in fifty-two-degree water to benefit the Provincetown Swim for Life. We meant not to convey approval of any particular behavior but to manifest the love of Christ for all types of people and to derive satisfaction from earning a few hundred dollars for AIDS relief in a small community with a very large health problem. We loved the people we met and appreciated their kindness to us in our near-hypothermic condition. Shivering men and women, straight and gay, healthy and lacking immunities, crowded close together[11] as we circled round and round under the single hot shower, persons created and loved by God.

From one blood he made every nation of mankind to dwell upon the face of the whole earth, and he allotted the times of their existence, and the boundaries of their habitations, so that they would search for God and perhaps feel around for him and find him—though indeed he is not far from each one of us. (Acts 17:26-27)

NOTES

1. Lawrence E. Stager, "Eroticism and Infanticide at Ashkelon," *Biblical Archaeology Review* 18 (July-Aug. 1991); n. 14.

2. Plato *Symposium* 191e; *Greek Anthology* 5.1108. Plutarch *Moralia* 769ef; 140e-143a. Lucian *Erotes* 27. Achilles Tatius *Leukippe and Cleithophon* 2.37-38.

3. Plutarch *Amores* 750C. See also Lucian *Erotes* 51, 39-40; *Anthologia Palatina* 12.245.

4. Aristophanes *Plutus* 155. Xenophon *Memorabilia* 1.6.13. Democritus Ep. 4.11; Phalaris Ep. 4, in *Epistolographi Graeci*, ed. R. Hercher (Amsterdam: A. M. Kahhert, 1965), p. 409.

5. Diogenes Laetius 7.173. Philo, e Ambrahamo 26. Lucius *Asinus* 37. Plutarch *Caius Gracchus* 4. Plautus *Miles Gloriosus* 668. Vettius Valens Astrolgus 2.36 (ed. W. Kroll; Berline, 1908), 113.22; Bettius Valens Astrologus 2.37 (ed. Kroll), 121.25-26. *See also* Ptolemy *Tetrobiblios* 14. Dio Cassius *Historicus* 58.4. Hibeh Papyri, part 1 (ed. B. P. Grenfell and A. S. Hunt; London, 1906). Pseudo-Aristotle *Problemata* 4.26. 880a-5; *see also* 879b21.

6. Hippolytus *Ref. Omn. Haer.* 5.28.22-23 (GCS 26, 130). Epigr. adesp. *Anthol. Pal.* 9.686.5. Rhetorius Aegyptius *Catalogus Codicum Astrologorum Graecorum* (CCAG) 8.4 p. Cod. 6, 8, ed. Par. gr. 2425 F.122) 196, 6, 8. *Sibylline Oracles* 2.73. Polycarp *To the Philippians* 5.3; Origen *de principiis* 7.12 (M. 17.181B). Johannes Malalas *Chronographia* 18 (M. 97.644A). Eusebius *demonstratio evangelica* 1.6 (M. 22.65C). Eusebius *Praepar. Evang.* 6.10 (M. 21.472A). Psuedo-*Historia ecclesiastica* 4.20 (M. 82.1169). Aristides *Apologia* 13.7. Goodspeed ap. John of Damascus 26-27 *Vita Barlaam et Joasaph* 27.96.860 (passages in Goodspeed cited from J. A. Robinson J 1 (1891) p. 100 fr. in P Lond 2486, ed. H.J.M. Milne JTS (1924 p. 75); Nilus of Ankara *epistularum libri quattuor*. 2.282 (M. 79.341A); Joannes Jejunator-Johannes IV Constinopolitanus (died 595), *poenitentiale* (M. 88.1893C). Cyril Alexandrinus *Homiliae diversae*. 14 (5.1.414C); 14.5.414 (ed. Aubert); Macarius Alexandrinus *hom.* 4.22 (M. 34.489B); Theophilus *Ad Autolycum* 1.2, 14.

7. Philo *Special Laws* 3.39. Testament of Naphtali 3:3-4; Wisdom of Solomon 14:25-26.

8. Scholion on Lucian *Dialogues of Prostitutes* 7.4.
9. Plutarch *Julius Caesar.*
10. Herodotus 2.46; Diodorus Siculus 1.85.
11. Yes, we were still wearing our bathing suits!

WHAT DOES THE BIBLE SAY ABOUT HOMOSEXUALITY?

Victor Paul Furnish

Chapter 2

T he writings of the Old and New Testaments are foundational for Christian faith and witness. They constitute, collectively, the church's Scripture. It is therefore imperative that the believing community seek the guidance of Scripture as it considers any subject like homosexuality. In doing so this community must (1) take care not to force these ancient writings to answer questions they do not address, (2) attend to the particular contexts—literary, cultural, historical, and religious—within and for which each biblical text was written, and (3) recognize *how* the Bible is authoritative for Christian faith and witness.

Questions Not Addressed

The distinction that one now routinely makes between heterosexuality and homosexuality was not made, and could not have been made, in the ancient world. Such a distinction presupposes understandings of sexuality, including sexual orientation, that emerged only toward the end of the nineteenth century. The word *homosexual* was not coined until 1869 (in German) to describe the theory, just then beginning to take shape, that from birth some people are affectionally predisposed toward persons of their own sex. Since the biblical languages (ancient Hebrew and Greek) had no words for *sexuality*, *heterosexuality*, or *homosexuality*, it is anachronistic and misleading when, as occasionally happens, the term *homosexual(s)* is used to translate some biblical expression.

Of course, what one today calls "homosexual" acts are attested in virtually all ancient cultures. In certain times and places, they were tacitly approved or even affirmed. In other times and places, they were judged to be degrading, polluting (for example, in ancient Israel and subsequently in Judaism), or unnatural (for example, by many moral philosophers contemporary with Jesus and Paul).[1] It was universally presupposed, however, that same-sex practices were simply a matter of preference. In biblical times, possible predisposing factors (whether genetic, social, or psychological) were not only unknown but quite beyond conceiving. The assumption was that people just chose (except in cases of rape) to have one kind of sex rather than the other, either occasionally or exclusively.[2] In the Bible, therefore, only sexual intercourse comes into view. There is nothing about sexual identity, sexual orientation, or the like. When one forces the Bible to address questions of which it has no conception, whatever answers one may get are not really *biblical* answers at all. And in the process, one has risked being distracted from the Bible's agenda.

Indeed, there are only a few places in the Bible where same-sex practices come into view, and they are widely scattered. Moreover, such practices are never the topic of extended discussion; one finds only passing references or allusions. Other matters stand far higher on the moral agenda of the Bible: deceitfulness, transgression of the rights of others or indifference to their needs, greed, sloth, self-interest, injustice in the marketplace, oppression of the weak, exploitation of the poor and needy, proud religious posturing, self-righteousness—and lust for those of the *opposite* sex. In comparison with these, same-sex lust and practices are of distinctly marginal concern in the biblical traditions and writings.

The Contexts

It is wrong to lift the scattered biblical references and allusions to same-sex practices from their respective contexts, lump them all together, and then proclaim them to be "the biblical teaching about homosexuality." This violates the integrity of the individual texts and the biblical witness as a whole. Each reference or allusion must be read in the light of its particular literary, cultural, and historical contexts, and with attention to any specifically religious convictions on which it may depend.

A survey of the passages most often discussed in relation to homosexuality will illustrate this point.

Genesis 1–2: the Creation accounts. It is often concluded from Genesis 1:26-28, a reference to God's creation of male and female for the purpose of procreation, that homosexuality is fundamentally perverse and sinful. Then Genesis 2:24, which comments that a man leaves his parents to become "one flesh" with a woman, is also invoked as implicitly condemning homosexuality. Both statements, however, are meant to explain *what is typical of humankind as a whole.* Neither is meant to regulate what *ought* to be, and neither takes into account the morality or immorality of possible exceptional cases, for example, divorce and remarriage after divorce. Same-sex practices and relationships lie entirely beyond the purview of these passages.[3]

Genesis 19:1-25: Lot's visitors and the men of Sodom (in Judg. 19, another version is told about Gibeah). Lot has offered lodging in his home to two strangers (who are actually angels in disguise). When the men of the city come to Lot's door demanding to have sex with his visitors, Lot offers them his virgin daughters instead. Even though the ruffians are not agreeable to his offer, Lot's guests manage to escape unharmed. The subsequent destruction of Sodom and Gomorrah is interpreted as God's judgment against the evil designs of Lot's neighbors.

This story is not told to condemn homosexuality, or even sexual lust in general, for in that case the story could not implicitly commend Lot's offering of his virgin daughters, which it does. The narrator's silence about this offer shows also his overall patriarchal viewpoint. Clearly, this story condemns those who violate the right of any stranger to be provided hospitality— a tradition deeply rooted in the culture of the ancient Near East.[4] Although this particular violation would have involved same-sex rape, that is incidental to the main point.

Eventually, Sodom did come to symbolize same-sex acts— hence the later coining of the words *sodomy* and *Sodomites.* But despite their appearance in some English translations, these terms are never employed in the Bible itself. In the Bible, Sodom is only a symbol for evil in general, and for the judgment that will be visited upon all who continue in it (thus Ezek. 16:49-50).

Leviticus 18:22; 20:13: two slightly different formulations of a statute prohibiting male same-sex intercourse. One says only that a male should not lie with another male "as with a woman" because it is an "abomination." The other goes farther, specifying that each of the males involved shall be put to death. Both versions stand within the so-called Holiness Code (Lev. 17–26), a collection of laws of widely varying date and origin. Some of these are regulations concerning particular festivals and holy days, while others specify what things are ritually clean and unclean. Still others are moral laws, like the famous commandment to love the neighbor as oneself (19:18).

The statute about same-sex intercourse is *not* one of the moral laws in this code. Rather, it is one of the laws that is concerned with ritual purity, with what is clean and unclean in a quite objective sense as distinct from spiritual or moral purity. According to the ancient Hebrew conception, purity means keeping like things together and unlike things separate. Where things that belong to different categories get mixed, each is thereby polluted. That is why the laws of Leviticus prohibit sowing two different kinds of seeds in one field, wearing two different kinds of fiber at once, crossbreeding livestock, cross-dressing, and so on. Such regulations presuppose that anything mixed is thereby polluted, impure, unclean.[5]

According to the Hebrew idiom used in Leviticus, when two males have intercourse, the one who takes the passive role "lies the lyings of a woman." This idiom alerts us to the conception that underlies the taboo: same-sex intercourse is viewed as a mixing of roles. Ancient Hebrew culture assigned the superior, active role to the male and the inferior, passive role to the female. Any departure from these cultural expectations was regarded as polluting. When one of the male partners was thus defiled, the whole relationship was judged to be perverted, and the other male was regarded as equally unclean. It is not the *morality* of male same-sex relationships with which these rules are concerned. Questions about what would be good, just, faithful, equitable, or loving are not raised. These particular rules make sense only where the concern is for what is ritually pure.

1 Corinthians 6:9; 1 Timothy 1:10: two lists of "wrongdoers."[6] Similar lists appear elsewhere in the New Testament, but no two are identical. They do not presume to list all or even the worst evils; they name only those practices most generally condemned as wrong. Among the ten types of wrongdoers identified in 1 Corinthians 6:9 are males who play the more passive role in same-sex intercourse and males who play the more active role. It is possible, but not certain, that the first term refers specifically to adolescent boy-prostitutes and the second to their customers. Only the second term appears in 1 Timothy 1:10. However, neither of these lists nor their respective contexts actually discuss same-sex practices, so it is impossible to know exactly what is in mind.

Romans 1:26-27: the most extensive biblical reference to same-sex practices. This is just one sentence in Greek, and it may be translated as follows:

> For this reason God gave them up to degrading passions, for just as their women exchanged natural intercourse for unnatural so also the men, abandoning natural intercourse with women, were consumed with passion for one another, men committing shameless acts with men and receiving in their own persons the penalty required by their error.

Here Paul simply takes it for granted that same-sex intercourse is unnatural and in every instance an expression of sexual lust. The point he wishes to establish is that such acts are among the symptoms of humanity's fundamental sin—which is refusing to acknowledge and give thanks to God (Rom. 1:21, referring to Gentiles; also 2:23-24, referring to Jews). Paul is not singling out any one group or vice as especially evil. On the contrary, he is emphasizing that "there is *no distinction,* since *all* have sinned and fall short of the glory of God" (3:22-23; emphasis added). In the following chapters, he proceeds to spell out his gospel of God's reconciling love, with which even the "ungodly" and God's "enemies" are graced (e.g., 5:6-11).

Paul's remark about same-sex intercourse is incidental to his main point in Romans 1:18–3:20 and to his exposition of God's grace in the following chapters. One must also consider the ideological background of his remark. What Paul says about same-sex practices is typical of what various moral philosophers in his day, especially the Stoics, were saying. That he was acquainted with their views, at least as they had influenced Hellenistic-Jewish thought, is beyond question. It is equally evident that he shared three commonly held presuppositions about same-sex acts: that people who perform them could have decided just as readily not to, that their performance is always and inevitably lustful, and that they are absolutely unnatural.

Other ancient sources, pagan, Jewish, and Christian, give two main reasons for describing same-sex intercourse as unnatural. First, it is a threat to the patriarchal structure of society. When practiced by men—so went the argument—one or both are demeaned by taking the role that is properly the woman's (inferior and passive); and when practiced by women, one or both are guilty of usurping the role that is properly the man's (superior and aggressive).[7] Second, same-sex intercourse is condemned as unnatural because, were everyone to opt for it, humankind would be doomed to extinction. Obviously, the first of these arguments has meaning only in cultures where gender roles are defined as they were in the ancient world; and the second is valid only if one shares the ancient belief that same-sex intercourse has, potentially, the same appeal for everyone.

Biblical Authority

The concrete moral teachings and directives of the Bible are part of the total scriptural witness, but they do not constitute its distinctive core. The biblical writings function as Scripture within the church because in and through them this believing community is in touch with the roots of its faith. This faith has its origin in God's enlivening, transforming love, as attested in the traditions of ancient Israel and, definitively, in the apostolic witness to Jesus as the Christ. The believing community experiences God's love as saving grace, which it receives as both a gift and a claim. Just as grace nourishes this community's faith, so it defines faith's task. For the community and for its individual members, to live by faith means to let God's grace find daily expression in the world. This, above all, is the word that the church hears in Scripture.

The concrete moral teachings and directives of Scripture may be affirmed as evidence of the concern, both in ancient Israel and in the early church, to be faithful to the gift and claim of God's grace. However, these specific moral counsels and rules are all conditioned, to one degree or another, by the particular cultural and historical context within and for which they were originally formulated.[8] To the same extent that they were specifically relevant in those particular times and places, they are less specifically relevant in other times and places, including our own.

What the biblical writings presuppose and direct about matters of sex and gender is especially problematic, due in part to the deeply rooted patriarchalism of ancient society. As noted above, in the story of Sodom, not the slightest question is raised about Lot's offering of his virgin daughters to the gang outside his door. The rape of Lot's daughters could have been tolerated but not the rape of his *male* visitors. Another example is offered by the biblical teachings about divorce and remarriage. The Old Testament law presupposes that a wife is her husband's property, and it provides that a man can divorce his wife essentially without cause and remarry as he wishes (Deut. 24:1-4). By comparison, the absolute prohibition of divorce and remarriage that is found in New Testament sayings attributed to Jesus accords the woman a higher status (Mark 10:2-12). But very soon some believers discovered that the strict rule about marriage was not always humane, and so allowance was made for exceptional cases (thus Matt. 5:31-32; 19:9). In this case, as in many others, the biblical traditions confirm the truth of the poet's observation that "new occasions teach new duties." What Scripture attests as unchanging is the reality of the gift and claim of God's grace, not the specific ways that God's grace should come to expression in the world.

How, then, can Scripture help to inform the mind of the modern church in the matter of homosexuality? Certainly not by what a few biblical traditions and writers happen to say or imply about same-sex intercourse. The presuppositions underlying these scattered references and allusions are no longer credible, given all that is being learned about human sexuality, including homosexuality.[9] New knowledge about the world and new realities within it require the believing community constantly to rethink what actions express God's grace and what actions do not. To accomplish this task in a way that is credible, the church must avail itself of the most recent findings and the keenest insights from all pertinent fields of inquiry. And to accomplish this task in a way that is appropriate to the gospel from which it lives, the church must test every proposed decision and action by the criterion implicit in Paul's appeal, "Let all that you do be done in love" (1 Cor. 16:14). It is the gospel of grace from which this appeal derives that truly distinguishes the witness of Scripture; and it is, finally, this gospel that must inform the decisions and shape the actions of the believing community in the matter of homosexuality.

NOTES

1. Representative studies include Harry A. Hoffner, "Incest, Sodomy, and Bestiality in the Ancient Near East," in *Orient and Occident: Essays in Honor of C. H. Gordon*, ed. Harry A. Hoffner (Kevelaer: Butzon & Bercker;

Neukirchen-Vluyn: Neukirchener Verlag, 1973), pp. 81-90; Saara Lilja, *Homosexuality in Republican and Augustan Rome,* Commentationes Humanarum Litterarum, no. 74 (Helsinki: Societas Scientiarum Fennica, 1983); Robin Scroggs, *The New Testament and Homosexuality: Contextual Background for Contemporary Debate* (Philadelphia: Fortress Press, 1983), pp. 17-98; Paul Veyne, "Homosexuality in Ancient Rome," in *Western Sexuality,* ed. Philippe Aries and André Béjin, trans. Anthony Forster (Oxford: Blackwell & Mott, 1985), pp. 36-39.

2. For documentation, see Victor Paul Furnish, *The Moral Teaching of Paul: Selected Issues,* 2nd rev. ed. (Nashville: Abingdon Press, 1985), pp. 58-67.

3. See Phyllis A. Bird, "Genesis 1-3 as a Source for a Contemporary Theology of Sexuality," *Ex Auditu* 3 (1987):31-44.

4. Similarly, Simon Parker, "The Hebrew Bible and Homosexuality," *Quarterly Review* 11 (1991):4-19.

5. For details, see L. William Countryman, *Dirt, Greed, and Sex: Sexual Ethics in the New Testament and Their Implications for Today* (Philadelphia: Fortress Press, 1988), pp. 11-65.

6. Discussions of these and other New Testament passages are offered by Scroggs, *The New Testament and Homosexuality,* pp. 99-122; Furnish, *The Moral Teaching of Paul,* pp. 67-81; Countryman, *Dirt, Greed, and Sex,* pp. 109-23; and Abraham Smith, "The New Testament and Homosexuality," *Quarterly Review* 11 (1992): 18-32.

7. See Bernadette J. Brooten, "Paul's Views on the Nature of Women and Female Homoeroticism," in *Immaculate and Powerful: The Female in Sacred Image and Social Reality,* ed. C. W. Atkinson et al., Harvard Women's Studies in Religion Series (Boston: Beacon Press, 1985), pp. 61-87.

8. A similar approach is taken by Gerald T. Sheppard, "The Use of Scripture Within the Christian Ethical Debate Concerning Same-Sex Oriented Persons," *Union Seminary Quarterly Review* 40 (1985): 13-35.

9. For example, biological factors must now be taken very seriously; see Chandler Burr, "Homosexuality and Biology," *Atlantic Monthly,* March 1993, pp. 47-65.

STUDY GUIDE

A primary point of departure in how Christians think theologically about homosexuality stems from the distinctly different ways the Bible is interpreted. Richard and Catherine Clark Kroeger understand that both Old and New Testaments explicitly forbid homosexual practices, while Victor Paul Furnish argues that biblical writers did not even make "the distinction that one now routinely makes between heterosexuality and homosexuality."

The Kroegers stress the Creation stories as being normative for Christians, emphasizing that God created males and females for sexual union and marriage. Scattered biblical references and allusions, notes Furnish, do not constitute "the biblical teaching about homosexuality." He underscores the total scriptural witness of God's concern for justice and grace.

Items for Reflection

1. Do you think it is important to understand the cultural situation in which the writers of the Bible lived? Or are the words true in all places and at all times so that context makes no difference?

2. How do you use the Bible in decision making about other controversial, sexually related subjects (such as divorce)?

3. How do you think we are to interpret the Bible, especially stories from Genesis, in a scientific world?

4. What weight or importance do you give to the scriptural passages from Leviticus and Paul? How do you feel about the absence of any direct teachings of Jesus in regard to homosexuality?

SUGGESTED RESOURCES

Countryman, L. William. *Dirt, Greed, and Sex: Sexual Ethics in the New Testament and Their Implications for Today.* Philadelphia: Fortress Press, 1988. The significance of a purity ethic and a propriety ethic on contemporary interpretations of acceptable sexual norms is examined.

Furnish, Victor Paul. "Homosexuality." In *Harper's Bible Dictionary,* p. 402. San Francisco: Harper & Row, 1985. Also see *The Moral Teachings of Paul: Selected Issues.* 2nd ed. rev. Nashville: Abingdon Press, 1985.

Hays, Richard B. "Awaiting the Redemption of Our Bodies." *Sojourners,* July 1991, pp. 17-21. Argues that while "only a few biblical texts speak of homoerotic activity, all of them express unqualified disapproval."

Scroggs, Robin. *The New Testament and Homosexuality: Contextual Background for Contemporary Debate.* Philadelphia: Fortress Press, 1983. Scholarly liberal perspective.

Yamamoto, J. Isamu, ed. *The Crisis of Homosexuality.* Wheaton, Ill.: Victor Books, 1990. Used by those who argue a traditional stance against homosexuality.

CHAPTER 3

WHAT DOES SCIENCE TEACH ABOUT HUMAN SEXUALITY?

Joseph Nicolosi

Chapter 3

Scientific findings on homosexuality tend to focus in two areas: the biological factors and the psychological factors. Biological arguments tend to imply that persons are innately gay—that certain biological, genetic, or physiological factors with which one is born determine homosexuality. Psychological arguments, on the other hand, tend to emphasize the learned components of homosexuality, such as family patterns and role modeling that may predispose a person toward homosexuality. Recently, we have begun to realize that biology and psychology cannot be so neatly separated but are inseparably linked.

Biological Factors

That having been said, any discussion of the biological causes of homosexuality must begin with the caution that such findings are of a *correlational* nature; that is, science finds certain genetic and physiological factors associated with homosexuality, but we are hard-pressed to responsibly attribute a causal direction—we do not know which comes first.

As we shall see, there is evidence that biological factors (such as temperament) possibly predispose a person to homosexuality, but the evidence is strong that biology does not absolutely determine homosexuality. The implication of this for clergypersons, clinicians, educators, parents, and any interested adults will become apparent as this discussion unfolds.

Biological research has tended to study possible genetic, hormonal and, most recently, brain structure factors related to homosexuality. One of the first and most obvious lines of reasoning has involved the idea that homosexuality may be related to abnormally low levels of male hormones such as testosterone known to produce the bodily and behavioral changes associated with maleness (heightened sex drive, aggressivity, musculature, physical strength, etc.).

Some early human studies reported consistent and different hormonal patterns between heterosexual and homosexual men.[1] However, the studies were not convincing, lacked experimental consistency, and could not be repeated by other researchers.

D. J. West examined the possibility that male homosexuality was linked to unusually low levels of male hormones and concluded that deficiencies of androgens in adult men diminished the sensitivity and reactivity of the sexual apparatus, reduced lust, and eventually produced physical impotence but did not abolish heterosexuality.[2]

Furthermore, West observed that changes in male hormone levels large enough to produce feminine physiological characteristics (e.g., breast enlargement) did not as a rule alter males' sexual orientation.

Limited studies with rats[3] showed that altering the hormonal levels consistently produced homosexual behavior; however, the application of these findings to humans is limited. Psychologists, clerics, scientists, parents, and educators would all agree that to generalize from the behavior of rodents would be to reduce the human sexual experience to a level much lower than we know that experience to be. From the theological perspective, we could call sexuality "God's good gift"; from a psychotherapeutic perspective, it is a biosocial behavior important to human well-being and integrated sense of self.

Causes are multiple and complex. Science confirms the complexity of the human sexual response as a phenomenon that is indeed bigger than the sum of its biogenetic parts. As West has suggested, in higher animals and particularly in humans, sexual behavior ceases to be directly and immediately dependent upon hormone concentrations at any given moment. Researchers on sexuality again and again have confirmed that the human sexual response is, more appropriately, a complicated set of physiological, genetic, and learned responses to internal and external cues.

J. Tabin calls to mind the case of the hermaphroditic child (a child born with some physical sex characteristics of both sexes) as a naturally occurring test group able to shed light on this classic question of whether one is born gay or learns to be gay.[4]

In the hermaphroditic child, we may assume some genetic disturbance to be at the core of the altered or mixed physiological characteristics. As Tabin describes, in such cases, the doctor often makes a sex assignment at birth, and parents are instructed to raise the child in every way as a boy or a girl, depending on the selected designation. These early assignments of gender are made randomly and in some instances in opposition to the gender that is more strongly indicated biologically.

Tabin notes that these children developed a complete identification with their assigned sex, even so far as to growing up to marry and mate in a way appropriate to the assigned sex rather than the biologically predisposed gender.

This sort of work suggests the overriding influence and impact of parental cues and parentally transmitted sex roles in the formation of gender-linked behavior and sexual orientation.

Simon LeVay, working in La Jolla, California, published findings that suggested there were structural differences between homosexual and heterosexual persons in a very small part of the brain's hypothalamus.[5] LeVay proposed that this area, deep in the brain stem, was smaller in male homosexual human cadavers.

LeVay's findings were seen as particularly significant in that the hypothalamus is one of the brain's most primitive fight-flight structures and is responsible for such behaviors as sexual arousal, aggressivity, and general sensitivity to stimuli—behaviors with undeniable implications for male- and female-typed behaviors.

LeVay's finding was immediately taken as proof positive that people are innately homosexual or heterosexual. However, we must consider that his study was done on a very limited sample (nineteen gay men, all of whom died of AIDS), that analyses were made on cadavers, and that the division of the men in terms of homosexuality and heterosexuality was made after the fact on the basis of limited personal history. Further, the interstitial area isolated by LeVay as being smaller in homosexual persons is not much larger than a grain of sand and is therefore difficult to measure.

The LeVay study reminds us that any sort of conclusions about the brain differences between homosexual and heterosexual persons cannot be evaluated without noting the old chicken-or-the-egg dilemma strongly suggested by physiological psychology: functional change (that is, how we act, how a biological system is repeatedly used) can cause structural changes in the system. Thus, whether the hypothalamus changed as a result of a lifetime of homosexual behavior remains to be proven. Dr. Lewis Baxter and colleagues at UCLA have obtained the first direct evidence that successful behavior therapy can over time produce long-term changes in brain circuitry, leaning us toward the idea that experience can alter biological structure.[6]

Such studies suggest at least the possibility that certain behaviors (or psychological conditions, including homosexuality) may cause observable structural brain changes. As Byne and Parsons (1993) have said, "Because experience can alter the physiology and structure of the brain, the meaning of the word 'biologic' is somewhat ambiguous." That means a biological outcome does not necessarily mean a biological cause.

In terms of LeVay's findings then, we cannot ignore the possibility that behavior (twenty years in the gay life-style) could cause neurological changes in the activity center of the brain rather than these neurological brain conditions being the cause of homosexuality.

No Definitive Answer About Causality

At best this debate and recent findings like Baxter's must leave any responsible clinician, cleric, educator, concerned adult, or parent open to the idea that we cannot know which comes first, the brain phenomenon of homosexuality (if, in fact, there is such a brain phenomenon) or the behavior. Clearly, the idea that behavior alters structure is the less fixed or closed position. If behavior may alter structure rather than structure just occurring outside our control, individuals retain an element of free choice to responsibly choose or "unchoose" the gay life-style.

Other quasi-scientific arguments offered in defense of innate homosexuality center on the natural and constant recurrence of homosexuality in cultures and species over time. People who argue that individuals are born gay point to naturally occurring homosexuality in the animal world. However, W. Gadpaille explains, "Preferential homosexuality is not found naturally in any infrahuman mammalian species. Masculine/feminine differences and heterosexual preferences are quite consistent."[7]

Proponents of the innate homosexuality position also use the "magical" 10 percent figure. Popular media and even the American Psychological Association have adopted this 10 percent figure first published by sex researcher Alfred Kinsey. This supposedly consistent 10 percent homosexuality across time and cultures is offered up as yet more evidence that homosexuality is biologically based.

In fact, recent studies show a much lower and more variable rate of homosexuality. The National Opinion Research Center in Chicago in 1989 and 1992 reported a 2.8 percent incidence; Dr. Irving Bieber's extensive analytic study placed the figure at 1 to 2 percent; a 1989 Danish study of over three thousand randomly selected adults reported a 3 percent rate of male homosexual persons.[8]

The next question that science raises in trying to unravel the issue of innate versus learned homosexuality is: What species-promoting function might a gene for homosexuality have; why might the process of natural selection be predisposing a population toward a consistent percentage of gay individuals? The heterosexual gene might be understood in the context of natural selection for propagation of the species, but what might the species-promoting function of a homosexual gene be?

Gay activitist writers have suggested some sociohistorical rather than strictly scientific species-promoting functions for homosexuality. As these functions reflect values that shift from accepted norms, it is important for theologians, clinicians, educators, concerned adults, and parents to remain informed, clear but nonjudgmental with respect to them.

Some of these positions assert that male homosexual persons offer a contribution of what is dubbed "gay sentiment," a particular aesthetic view and heightened sensitivity that so-called straights lack. Some suggest the benefits of a third sex, having a woman's mind in a man's body (or vice versa for lesbians). This, it is suggested, might be a more highly evolved, androgynous personality structure that in some fashion announces a brave new world. Other defenders of the homosexual life-style suggest that removed from the entanglements of family and children, gay people have a special lesson to offer straights on the impracticability of being monogamous or of having one person satisfy all our emotional and sexual needs.

Homosexuality as Learned Behavior

In the end, we must take our lead in this innate versus learned question from scientific findings. Byne et al. have reviewed all the current physiological studies, and they conclude that there is no evidence at present to substantiate a biologic theory.[9] They point out that the recent twin studies, including those much touted recent studies of Bailey and Pillard and King and McDonald, are intriguing because of the large proportion of identical twins who were *not* both homosexual. If homosexuality is

genetic, identical twins should in every case be uniformly homosexual.

Byne et al. suggest an alternative to the biological model,
whereby temperament and personality traits interact with family
and social environment to produce sexual orientation. They
describe the literature as reviewed by van den Aardweg: "Many,
perhaps a majority of homosexual men report family constella-
tions similar to those suggested by Bieber et al. . . . e.g., over-
involved, anxious, controlling mothers, poor father-son relationships."[10]

Byne et al. propose an interactional model in which genes or
hormones do not specify sexual orientation per se but instead
predispose the individual through particular personality traits
to react in a specific way to parental and social influences. They
offer the example of a boy who is more likely to need the support
of maternal approval and less likely to seek male role models
outside the family. In the absence of encouragement from an
accepting father or alternative role model, such a boy would be
likely to feel different from his male peers and feel low masculine self-regard, isolation, and rejection, which could lead to an
eroticization of maleness.

Physiological factors may, therefore, predispose a man toward
male gender deficit in the same fashion that certain persons are
more prone to alcoholism than others. However, in neither case
do physiogenetic factors predetermine the condition. As a reparative psychotherapist, my orientation and concerns with respect to
understanding homosexuality lean toward the psychological.

The Nature of Therapy

Day in and day out, men of all ages present themselves at my
office in acute psychic discomfort over their homosexuality. In
most of these individuals I find homosexual fantasies and considerable homosexual acting out, but with a profound psychological discomfort about the idea of adopting and living a gay
life. Part of the ethics of my clinical practice is to respect the
patient's choice to strive to be free of his unwanted homosexu-

ality. My job is then one of two approaches, depending on the ultimate decision of the patient. I may refer him to a gay-affirmative psychologist if he decides to strive to integrate a homosexual identity (which rarely occurs in my particular practice, given my clear reputation as a reparative therapist). More often I help the patient who is committed to change see his homosexuality as a sort of false self ingrained from such an early and primitive stage of ego development that it has indeed felt like an innate condition.

In reviewing the family histories of homosexual men who seek my assistance (and this is an admittedly biased sample in that they come to me knowing that I specialize in reparative therapy), I find again and again, almost without fail, men who from a very early age were prevented from achieving a healthy identification with the male role. I consistently see the combination of an emotionally or physically removed father figure and an intensely, if lovingly, involved mother figure.[11]

The reason that homosexual men feel as if they were born gay is that the stage for homosexuality seems to be set at a very early phase of gender identity and early ego development. The prehomosexual boy experiences at some critical and psychologically formative stage of development a hurt or disappointment in his relationship with his father. The hurt may be the result of active abuse or simple neglect; many of these fathers are simply emotionally unavailable by disposition and if counseled wisely at the right stage in their sons' lives would have attempted to meet their needs for masculine identification. Others (these are more the rule than the exception) are so emotionally closed and self-involved that they cannot connect with their sons in any real way, even when their sons actively engage them emotionally in joint therapy sessions.

If overtures by the prehomosexual boy toward the father are continually ignored or rejected, there is a stage of protest, active revolt, and disruptive behavior toward the father. Then as a protection against future hurt, the prehomosexual boy detaches from the father. In case after case in my office I find that this protective stance takes the form of "never again—I reject you and what you represent"—namely, masculinity.

Later in childhood, the prehomosexual boy will indirectly express his anger by ignoring the father and denying that he has any importance in the family. The boy then forms an unusually close relationship with the mother against the father. Relatively healthy fathers who attempt at this stage to make reparative overtures—however awkward—are repeatedly rebuked. So deep is the early break in this male-to-male connection that nothing the father ever does again is right. Again and again, my patients recall their fathers as simply "not being there."

As a way of defending himself from further pain, the prehomosexual boy isolates himself from other males and from his own masculinity. Females are familiar, while males are both mysterious and rejecting. Then when sexual needs begin to seek expression in early adolescence, these interests will be away from the familiar and toward the unapproachable (the masculine). We do not sexualize what we are familiar with. We are drawn to the "other than me."

Understanding and treatment of ambivalent homosexuality from a reparative standpoint involves helping to put issues of early development in focus. Reparative therapy of homosexuality does not imply a magic cure; its goal is to improve a man's way of relating to other men and to strengthen masculine identification. In this fashion, the desire for closeness to a male—which when satisfied leads to appropriate male gender identification—may be readdressed by the patient in an accepting and protected arena. This, then, reestablishes the very process that was interrupted in the client's early childhood.

Ethical Concerns

What should get the attention of clerics, clinicians, educators, parents, and all concerned is not the eradication of homosexuality, because such a stance is intolerant and inhumane. What should at least engage our imagination, however, is the particular way the militant gay position turns homosexuality into a trivialized yet somehow irrefutable given. The gay-for-life-and-loving-it platform and the political and subcultural pressure for society to adopt this position have the effect of setting homosexuality in stone so to speak, regimenting homosexual men into a certain gay life-style. If society convinces him he cannot change, the homosexual individual is left no choice but to come out, donning the lingo and costume of the gay life-style, because the implicit message is that one is gay by birth, had better be happy to be gay, and that is that.

Reparative therapy allows a space wherein homosexual men seeking to do so may make a reasoned and judicious life-style choice to leave behind both the gay world and the political and subcultural pressure to espouse it.

The recent use of science as proof positive for the born gay position has been damaging to the self-determination of gay men and women. If people are born gay, it is presumed they cannot change, and this forces therapists, clergypersons, parents, educators, and friends to abdicate their potential role as change facilitators. Input would then be limited to compassionate support and nurturing acceptance. For many men and women, this is not enough: they seek to grow beyond the homosexual predicament.

NOTES

1. G. Dorner, W. Rohde, F. Stahl, L. Krell, and W. Masins, "A Neuroendocrine Predisposition for Homosexuality in Men," *Archives of Sexual Behavior* 4 (1975):1-7.

2. D. J. West, *Homosexuality Re-examined* (Minneapolis: University of Minnesota Press, 1977).

3. Ibid., pp. 64-65.

4. J. Tabin, *On the Way to the Self* (New York: Columbia University Press, 1985), pp. 38-39.

5. S. LeVay, "A Difference in Hypothalmic Structure Between Heterosexual and Homosexual Men," *Science* 253 (Aug. 30, 1991):956-60.

6. Joseph Nicolosi, "Functional Change Causes Structural Change," National Association for Research and Therapy of Homosexuality (NARTH) newsletter, Encino, Calif., December 1992, pp. 1-2.

7. W. Gadpaille, "Cross Species and Cross Cultural Contributions to Understanding Homosexual Activity," *Archives of General Psychiatry* 37 (1980):349-56.

8. J. Nicolosi, ed., "The 10% Myth," *NARTH (National Association for Research and Therapy of Homosexuality newsletter)*, March 1993.

9. W. Byne et al., "Human Sexual Orientation: The Biologic Theories Reappraised," *Archives of General Psychiatry* 50, 3 (March 1993): 228-39.

10. Ibid.

11. J. Nicolosi, *Reparative Therapy of Male Homosexuality* (Northvale, N.J.: Jason Aronson, 1991).

WHAT DOES SCIENCE TEACH ABOUT HUMAN SEXUALITY?

Ruth L. Fuller

Chapter 3

What Is Science?

I n our Western/Euro-American culture of the 1990s, persons often refer to findings of science as if they were speaking of a culture-free, value-free system of thought. Furthermore, most persons assume the facts used by one scientist can be reproduced by other scientists. If one considers the worldwide history of knowledge, this culturally determined, and therefore culturally limited, picture of scientific thought is a relatively recent development. Yet in the Euro-American setting, most of us are not accustomed to viewing scientific information as limited by the cultural biases of investigators and/or institutions.[1]

For example, our limited view may negate any critical examination of the ways in which the values of scientists can unintentionally distort the facts. Since most scientists are Anglo, male, and heterosexual, their perspectives dominate the literature.

A historical review of attempts to cure behaviors deemed by a particular culture as abnormal indicates we have tried to cure or eliminate various behaviors or qualities on the basis of sex, handedness, size, race, physical or mental disabilities, and sexual orientation.[2] Even the history of our Judeo-Christian, Euro-

American heritage reflects this tendency. Prior to our current Latin-derived meanings, homosexuality also included sex with subhuman Gentiles and Muslims and animals.[3]

In the late nineteenth century, Western medical science was dominated by middle-class Victorian men looking for expanded power and higher community status. They developed the degeneracy theory, a linkage of pathology with poverty, alcoholism, and crime. Physicians adhering to this theory enhanced their role in regulating the moral life of the community. Mendelian genetics and Darwin's survival of the fittest doctrine were used to reenforce the degeneracy theory. During that period of time, homosexuality was defined as pathological.[4]

Another cultural complexity in Western society is our tendency to dismiss traditional wisdom as primitive superstition. Earlier in history, our physical, social, and emotional worlds were clearly defined as unknowable, or divinely ordained. Our contemporary view requires commitment to explanations of human behavior that are objective or scientific rather than traditional. In spite of our professed commitment to science, the interplay between traditional wisdom and scientific truth affects the escalating, passionate discourses on homosexuality.

What Is Homosexuality?

Manipulations of either tradition or science are required to make science fit the many religious groups' traditional teachings about homosexuality.

Definitions

Chandler Burr reminds us that the word *homosexual* appeared for the first time in Euro-American literature in the 1860s when modern (Western) medicine developed an interest in the subject.[5] Today homosexuality has simpler and more complex definitions that require an expanded vocabulary.

The simplified definition used by most nonscientists is "the sexual desire for a person or persons of the same sex as oneself."[6] This simplicity of definition implies uniformity in the experience of persons so defined. For approximately one hundred years, Western medicine in general and psychiatry in particular used this definiton and declared sexual desire for a person of the same sex as pathological, an illness. In 1973, the American Psychiatric Association concluded that there was no scientific basis for this one hundred-year-old declaration. The association's conclusion is based on two critical factors: (1) lack of evidence of any maladaptive behavior that is exclusively homosexual, and (2) lack of evidence that *all* homosexual persons are maladapted.[7]

The subsequent twenty years have seen a continuous evolution in our understanding of what is called homosexuality. Based on cumulative research and evidence, the American Psychoanalytic Association passed a resolution in 1992 that persons of same-sex orientation are no longer excluded from training for status as analysts because of sexual orientation. Each is to be judged on individual merit, just as all other candidates are judged.

The assumed homogeneity of homosexuality continues to be a misconception that is generally omitted in religious and secular discussions of the subject. Among others, Warren J. Gadpaille outlines a more complex but clear series of definitions of the "varieties of homosexual (same sex) expression."[8] It is helpful to look at these definitions from the point of view of the life cycle of human development. This point of view acknowledges a multidimensional interplay of dynamic, complex factors including (1) biological components (genetic, nutritional, hormonal, etc.), (2) psychological functioning, (3) the sociological organization of the environment, and (4) the content of cultural factors taken in geographical and historical context.[9]

The varieties of homosexual expression include *developmental homoerotic activity* in children and adolescents of both sexes before adulthood (a developmental view that children and adolescents are immature in their expressions of sexuality); *pseudohomosexuality* in which the sexual activity with persons of the same sex reflects issues of dependence-independence and/or power-powerlessness rather than sexual desire, e.g., two females whose focus is a mother-child relationship of nurture rather than one of sexual arousal for satisfaction; *situational homosexuality* in captive same-sex populations during the time of their isolation from persons of the opposite sex, e.g., jail and prison populations; *enforced/exploitative homosexuality,* complementary sexual activities in which a less powerful individual is exploited by a more powerful individual; *variational homosexuality,* e.g., prostitution; *bisexuality,* in which a homosexual person continues to have heterosexual relations, and a smaller group of persons who present *ambisexuality,* equal sexual pleasure and performance with either sex; *ideological or political homosexuality,* e.g., women who see sex with a man as a capitulation to the enemy; and *preferential or exclusive homosexuality,* adults whose emotional and physical responses to persons of the same sex are preferred when there are no restrictions on availability of potential partners. There is the incorrect assumption that preferential or exclusive homosexuality presents no diversity. The diversity includes persons who are *asexual or celibate, nonmonogamous singles,* and *couples.*[10]

Sociocultural Factors

In a historical cross-cultural view, there are cultures in which same-sex sexual activity is considered to be normative. For example, in some Western, Native American, Mediterranean, Latin American, Pacific, and African cultures, same-sex activity is related to the establishment and/or maintenance of power, the enjoyment of beauty, or the rites of passage into adulthood.[11] The historical argument that such same-sex expressions are primitive and therefore irrelevant, at best, and wrong and/or sinful, at worst, reflects the traditional stance of this culture toward the highly charged issues of cultural diversity and human sexuality.

As research in all of these fields increases, the psychological, sociological, anthropological, and philosophical milieus in which human beings develop become better understood as the diverse, dynamic, complex systems that they are.

Biological Factors

Human beings are one of the wonders of the physical universe. The explosion of information about our physical selves, our physical environment, and the interplay between them has given rise to an ever-increasing scientific vocabulary that makes the vocabulary of forty or fifty years ago seem quaint, similar to a child of the 1990s viewing airplanes with propellers. We have moved along a potentially mind-boggling spectrum that includes anatomy, biochemistry, biophysics, cell biology, neurobiology, physiology, neurophysiology, endocrinology, genetics, molecular biology, psychoendocrinology, and ethnopsychophysiology (the study of the additional factor of ethnicity in the psychophysiological functioning of individuals). Each of these specialties has relevance to any discussion of homosexuality. Burr underscores the overlapping nature of the fields of research that are necessary in order to pursue such complex (neuro-bio-psycho-socio-cultural) phenomena as sexual orientation (1980s) or sexual preference (pre-1980s).[12]

In March 1993, many persons anticipated that research was close to defining a gene for or multiple genetic sites influencing the presentation of homosexuality. A July 1993 report in *Science* notes the discovery of the gene. Replication of the research is awaited with more than casual interest.[13] It may be that in the very foreseeable future one piece of this multifactorial equation will be clearer. Nevertheless, proponents of an argument either for or against nature have not attended to the complexity of multifactorial thinking.[14]

Causality and Homosexuality

Since culture influences the questions science addresses at a given time in history, it is useful to ask, Why the great interest in the causes of homosexuality at this time? Are there similar interests in the causes of heterosexuality, asexuality, or celibacy? The reasons for our collective interest now are not purely scientific. This culture frequently has pursued justification for the maltreatment of persons deemed ill, deviant, or subhuman. Those labeled deviant are fewer in number and possess less in power than other members of the society in which they live.[15] For persons to feel they are insiders in a society, another group of persons must be assigned the role of outsider. It seems our interest in the causes and cures of homosexuality addresses our current societal need for outsiders.

We are still working on establishing culture-free questions about homosexuality that can be pursued to more objective answers. Given the current status of this complex subject and the incomplete information available, a definitive answer about cause is not available.

Serious studies of the "how, when, why, and wherefore" of sexuality in general and homosexuality in particular have been prospective and long term. Richard Green's report on his fifteen-year prospective study of two groups of boys (initially engaged in the study at ages four to eleven) gives insight into the development of homosexuality or bisexuality in boys presenting the "sissy boy syndrome." To be in the study, the boys' behavior included saying that they wanted to be girls, preferring to play with dolls as a favorite toy, dressing in girls' clothes often, and avoiding rough sports. The matched group of controls did not present these behaviors. Fifteen years later, 75 percent of the study group of boys were homosexual or bisexual. In the control group, one member was homosexual or bisexual. Green noted that when psychological treatment was pursued to change these behaviors it did not harm the participants. On the other hand, the treatment made no difference in the outcome of the sexuality.[16]

In looking at the development of sexual identity and sexual orientation, one might wonder if these observations at the ages of four to eleven were early, late, or timely. The observations were not too early. With decades of collective, prospective work, researchers such as Katz, Roiphe, and Galenson look at infants (below age one) and toddlers who already evidence a clear sense of their gender by age two.[17]

It is in this area of infant development (below age one to age three) that scientists have been most aware of what we do not know. The rainbow spectrum of normal development, factors impeding or creating diversity in development, and factors of resiliency may add a helpful contribution to the understanding of sexual identity and orientation.[18]

On Changing Orientation

The difficulty in addressing the question of changing orientation (as compared to preference) is related to the issue of causes. If homosexuality is a genetically determined orientation, it is as likely to be changed as skin color! (There are over two hundred genes that influence skin color. Knowing the cause of skin shades seems to have had little effect on racism, which leads one to wonder whether determination of cause will have much effect on the culture's acceptance of homosexuality.)

Psychological features may be relevant to change of orientation. Internal conflict and unhappiness that interfere with a person's growth and development are powerful forces. In some cases a person's pain may be related to sexual orientation or preference and may evoke a desire for change. Since most therapists focus in specialized areas, there are those who focus on patients whose sexual orientation is problematic for their well-being.

Patients tend to select clinicians who espouse a compatible viewpoint, asking,[19] for example, "Are you a Christian therapist?" Therefore, clinicians will speak from their experience with a selected sample, sometimes generalizing assumptions for the total population that may be true for only a small segment of persons who happen to choose a particular type of therapy.

Few of the gay and lesbian individuals I have seen in the last thirty years came about changing their sexual orientation. Most came in pain about relationships or the loss of an important relationship. The choice of seeing me as compared to other potential psychiatrists or other therapists was most often based on ethno-cultural compatibility and a clinical reputation for being able to formulate goals *with* the person or family coming in rather than *for* them. I, too, have a biased sample of the population.

Looking for Cures to a Nondisease

The American Psychoanalytic Association is taking the position that homosexuality is not a disease and does not exclude potential applicants from pursuing analytic training.

Unfortunately history records biological treatments of homosexuality including surgical castration and hysterectomy as well as harsh psychological treatments based on shame and guilt. Currently, evidence suggests that psychological treatment can help a person sort out and rework the pains of being treated as the outsider because of same-sex orientation. Such treatment has been helpful in making the individual's environment less hostile and in increasing the person's self-esteem. Some clinicians believe psychological treatments to change orientation apparently do no obvious harm and are appropriate.[20] Other clinicians believe such treatment does serious damage.[21]

Future Issues

Our scientific efforts in the combined fields of genetics and molecular biology have raised the recurrent question of genetic, cellular, and perhaps molecular manipulation.[22] If any or all of the multiple factors related to homosexuality can be manipulated, how would such manipulation be accomplished? Determined by whom? For what purpose(s)?

Homosexuality is a politically charged subject that has risen on our cultural hit parade to one of the top slots. In sweeping stereotypical indictments, any person to whom this pejorative sexual label is attached is assumed to be promiscuous, pedophilic, assaultive or deserving to be assaulted, criminal, and so on. Burr reminds us that science will not answer questions about societal responsibilities to its members, ethics, and human rights.[23]

NOTES

1. Sally B. Geis and Ruth L. Fuller, "Inadvertent Discrimination in Medical Research," *Religion and Health* 29 (1990):207-17. See also Paul Pederson, ed., *Handbook of Cross-Cultural Counseling and Therapy* (New York: Praeger, 1987), pp. xv, 336.

2. Vincent Collins, M.D., "Cross-Cultural Psychiatry: Some Clinical Observations," University of Colorado Health Sciences Center, Department of Psychiatry, Division of Child Psychiatry, Grand Rounds, Nov. 1, 1985.

3. Chandler Burr, "Homosexuality and Biology," *Atlantic Monthly*, March 1993, pp. 48-49.

4. David F. Greenberg, *The Social Construction of Homosexuality* (Chicago: University of Chicago Press, 1988), pp. 413-21.

5. Burr, "Homosexuality and Biology," p. 48.

6. *Webster's Dictionary*, p. 647.

7. American Psychiatric Association, *Diagnostic and Statistical Manual of Mental Disorders* (DSM-III-R), 3d ed., rev. (Washington, D.C.: American Psychiatric Association, 1987), pp. 290-96. Lists the sexual disorders that do not include homosexuality.

8. Warren J. Gadpaille, M.D., "Homosexuality," in *Understanding Human Behavior in Health and Illness*, ed. Richard C. Simons, M.D., 3d ed. (Baltimore: Williams & Wilkins, 1985), pp. 391-401.

9. Ruth L. Fuller, "Mental Health Educational Processes for Minority (Black) Populations," in *Minority Mental Health Education Processes: A Report of a Workshop* (Center for Clinical Personnel Development, Division of Human Resources, National Institute of Mental Health, 1984), pp. 142-79. See also Howard M. Bahr, "Family Change and the Mystique of the Traditional Family," in *Families in Transition: Primary Prevention Programs that Work*, ed. Lynne A. Bond and Barry M. Wagner (Newbury Park, Calif.: SAGE Publications, 1988), pp. 13-40, copyright by the Vermont Conference on the Primary Prevention of Psychopathology.

10. Gadpaille, "Homosexuality," in *Understanding*, pp. 391-401.

11. Luis A. Vargas and Joan D. Koss-Chicino, eds., *Working With Culture: Psychotherapeutic Interventions with Ethnic Minority Children and Adolescents* (San Francisco: Jossey-Bass Publishers, 1992), pp. 319, 323.

12. Burr, "Homosexuality and Biology," p. 60.

13. "Evidence of Homosexuality Gene," *Science*, July 16, 1993, pp. 291-92.

14. Marshall H. Segall, "Psychocultural Antecedents of Male Aggression: Some Implications Involving Gender, Parenting, and Adolescence" in *Health and Cross-Cultural Psychology: Towards Applications*, eds. Pierre R. Dasen, John W. Berry, and Norman Sartorius (Newbury Park, Calif.: SAGE Publications, 1988), pp. 71-93.

15. Ruth L. Fuller, Sally B. Geis, and Julian Rush, "Lovers of AIDS Victims: A Minority Group Experience," *Death Studies* 12 (1988):1-7.

16. Richard Green, M.D., *The "Sissy Boy Syndrome" and the Development of Homosexuality* (New Haven, Conn.: Yale University Press, 1987), pp. 318-19.

17. Phyllis Katz, Ph.D., personal communication, 1992; H. Roiphe and Eleanor Galenson, M.D., *Infantile Origins of Sexual Identity* (New York: International Universities Press, 1981), p. 19.

18. Paul Henry Mussen, John Janeway Conger, Jerome Kagan, and Aletha Carol Huston, *Child Development and Personality*, 7th ed. (New York: Harper & Row, 1990), pp. 590-92.

19. Elaine V. Siegel, Ph.D., "Severe Body Image Distortions in Some Female Homosexuals," *Dynamic Psychotherapy* 2 (Spring-Summer 1984):18-26.

20. Charles W. Socarides, "Sexual Politics and Scientific Logic: The Issue of Homosexuality," *The Journal of Psychohistory* (Winter 1992):317-20.

21. Richard A. Isay, *Being Homosexual* (New York: Straus & Giroux, 1989), pp. 61-66.

22. Sharon J. Durfy and Amy E. Grotevant, *The Human Genome Project*, Scope Note 17 (Washington, D.C.: National Reference Center for Bioethics Literature, Kennedy Institute of Ethics, Georgetown University, Dec. 1991).

23. Burr, "Homosexuality and Biology," pp. 61-62.

STUDY GUIDE

This chapter presents as accurately as possible the findings of the social and natural sciences regarding the complexities of human sexuality with special attention to gay and lesbian persons. Issues related to possible causality, nature versus nurture arguments, psychological and sociological dimensions, and health concerns are explored.

A major difference between the two essays emerges in the discussion about the possibilities for persons to change or be transformed from homosexual to heterosexual behavior. Nicolosi accents "reparative therapy" for gay men, while Fuller emphasizes the limits of this possibility as well as the complexity of the issue.

Items for Reflection

1. We know what causes skin color to vary among racial groups. Does knowing the cause make racism less prevalent or less painful? If we knew the cause of homosexuality, would that change attitudes?

2. If you consider yourself heterosexual, what do you think caused your attraction to the opposite sex?

3. Do you believe people can be changed or transformed from heterosexuality to homosexuality or vice versa? What conditions do you think are necessary?

4. Do you think science is purely objective and value free?

SUGGESTED RESOURCES

Bailey, J. M., and R. C. Pillard. "A General Study of Male Sexual Orientation." *Archives of General Psychiatry* 48 (1991):1089-1096.

Burr, Chandler. "Homosexuality and Biology." *Atlantic Monthly,* March 1993, pp. 47-65. A layperson's survey of the current status of scientific knowledge about homosexuality.

Falco, Kristine. *Psychotherapy with Lesbian Clients.* New York: Brunner/Mazel, 1991. An excellent resource exploring issues of identity, relationship, and other counseling concerns.

Isay, Richard A., M.D. *Being Homosexual.* New York: Straus & Giroux, 1989. A gay psychiatrist affirms acceptance of homosexuality.

Nicolosi, Joseph. *Reparative Therapy of Male Homosexuality.* Northvale, N.J.: Jason Aronson, 1991.

Socarides, Charles W., M.D. *Homosexuality: Psychoanalytic Therapy.* Northvale, N.J.: Jason Aronson, 1989. The author provides leadership to those who do not accept the current official American Psychiatric Association decision to define homosexuality as acceptable.

ARE CHRISTIANITY AND HOMOSEXUALITY INCOMPATIBLE?

Marva J. Dawn

What Is Christianity?

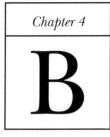

Chapter 4

Before asking if homosexuality is incompatible with Christianity, we must note Christianity's central truths and their implications for this discussion:

1. All are sinners needing a Savior. Therefore, Christians won't judge or castigate but must proclaim and incarnate God's love for each person. To condemn homosexuals is to deny one's own sexual vulnerability.

2. Blinded by sinful nature, humankind needs God's revelation to show us the truth about ourselves. Living in response to grace, however, Christians cannot reduce ethics simply to a system of rules.

3. Rather, biblical narratives nurture godly character in Christians. Building faithfulness in following Jesus, the community's discipleship offers alternatives to the idolatries of cultures rejecting God's principles.

What Is Homosexuality?

Many Christians, genuinely seeking to love, criticize biblical perspectives as horribly outmoded in light of what we now know about homosexuality. The church's historical stance advocating change or demanding lifelong celibacy seems inhumane and degrading.

Let's ask carefully what is known about homosexuality. Certainly, sexual/emotional experiences shape a person's erotic orientation. Such factors as prenatal hormones, genetics, dysfunctional parent-child relationships, and reinforcing experiences influence in varying degrees persons' understandings of their sexual identity. Scientists acknowledge that homosexuality cannot develop without learning and socialization.[1]

David Greenberg's massive sociological study, *The Construction of Homosexuality,* disproves the contemporary notion of an essential/natural static homosexuality as a biological condition or psychological orientation. His three-hundred-page overview of sexual patterns, behaviors, and ideas before modern times demonstrates instead that different cultures variously form and interpret sexual identity. Greenberg's general typology of homosexualities in primitive, kinship-structured societies (transgenerational, transgenderal, initiation-rite, cultic, and class-structured) and his descriptions of homosexual innovations in archaic civilizations display an enormous amount of examples against which the idea of a static homosexual essence cannot stand. There "was not 'a homosexual'—a distinct type of person—but someone who had engaged in a homosexual act."[2]

The second part of *The Construction of Homosexuality* demonstrates thoroughly how various factors have influenced the development of the modern homosexual identity—mechanistic understandings of behavior; competitive capitalism; the medicalization of homosexuality; urbanization; bureaucratization; and the loss of communal guidance and friendship intimacy. Greenberg concludes that any " 'essences' that structure erotic feelings" are "unstable or subject to environmental influence." Thus, the essentialist argument that homosexual persons can't change is rendered questionable as is the theory that homosexual teachers don't influence the sexual identity of their students.[3]

Greenberg's conclusions don't legitimize simplistic condemnations of homosexual persons or denial of their human rights and civil liberties, but his thorough research clarifies indisputably that nothing in science mandates a radical overhaul of the church's historical stance concerning homosexual acts. However, the church must ask new questions.[4]

What Fosters Homosexuality?

Many factors in our technological society augment the development of homosexual identity—hedonism; relaxed attitudes toward divorce, premarital sex, and pornography; feminism that rejects heterosexual "consorting with the enemy"; cultural relativism; delegitimation of accepted authority; skepticism about values and beliefs; sociology's concern with self-identity; gender confusions. Basically, our culture's inability to distinguish between social and genital sexuality, its genital idolatry because of the loss of family/community social supports, and its lack of skills for intimacy have destroyed the ultimate meaning of sexual intercourse. What alternatives can the church offer our world for friendship and for sexual understanding, chastity, and fulfillment?

What Does the Bible Actually Say?

Homosexuality debates are confused if biblical exegesis is not clearly separated from hermeneutics—if interpreting what the Scriptures actually say is muddled by what we *want* the Bible to say.[5] Christ's followers are different from the world around us in that our lives are formed by the revelation of God's design for humankind. Thus, our first ethical step is to discern as clearly as possible what God's Word says. Then we can ask better questions about applying scriptural accounts to our present-day care for homosexual persons.

Richard Hays carefully separates biblical study from application and thereby effectively reveals homosexuality as but one result of the radical rebellion of human beings against their

Creator. In the whole context of Romans 1, the apostle Paul's charge that

> fallen humans have "exchanged natural relations for unnatural" means nothing more nor less than that human beings, created for heterosexual companionship, as the Genesis story bears witness, have distorted even so basic a truth as their sexual identity by rejecting the male and female roles which are "naturally" theirs in God's created order.[6]

All the biblical references unambiguously indict homosexual behavior as a violation of God's intention for humanity.[7] Furthermore, Jewish and Christian literature through the Middle Ages never relaxed its opposition to homosexual behavior.[8] The difficult question is what bearing this normative/corrective tradition has for ethical thinking in the twentieth-century church.

How Does the Bible Apply?

The Bible doesn't simply forbid homosexual acts. Instead, from Genesis' creation of male and female through Ephesians' declaration that marriage symbolizes the mystery of God's faithfulness, it presents an overarching, consistent vision of God's beautiful design for human sexuality, expressed genitally only within the permanent commitment of heterosexual marriage. Gender identity is formed in the community of people who image God.

Ethically, even though we are shaped by forces beyond our control—genetics, physical conditions, parental influences, culture—the Bible holds us accountable for what we do with who we are. We shape ourselves by every decision, building who we become as women and men.

The Bible functions "as a diagnostic tool, laying bare the truth about humankind's dishonorable 'exchange' of the natural for the unnatural." Romans 1 shows that "homosexual relations, however they may be interpreted (or rationalized—cf. Romans 1:32) by fallen and confused creatures, represent a tragic distortion of the created order" (207). Consequently, the critical question is whether we grant the normative force of biblical analysis. Christian communities must be very clear: What sources authorize our conclusions about homosexuality?

Conflicts arise because contemporary homosexual persons claim the grace of God in their stable, loving relationships. How should we assess such claims? Hays asks, "Was Paul wrong? Or are such experiential claims simply another manifestation of the blindness and self-deception that Paul so chillingly describes? . . . Or are there new realities that Paul didn't know about?" (207).

Many contemporary theologians claim that God is "doing a new thing." A recent Society of Biblical Literature panelist, discussing homosexuality as a case issue in the use of biblical authority, suggested that, just as Paul overturned Israelite food purity laws for the sake of the church's unity, we should now set aside sexual purity laws. Her suggestion completely ignored the congruity of texts about homosexual practice with every biblical normative and descriptive passage about God's design for sexuality.

As Hays warns, deciding that other considerations finally outweigh the authority of biblical judgment against homosexuality must be done "with a due sense of the gravity of [that] choice." The theological structure of biblical indictments of relations "contrary to nature" is "indeed weighty," and "not explicitly counterbalanced by anything in Scripture or Christian tradition." Arguments favoring the acceptance of homosexual relations "find their strongest warrant in empirical investigation and contemporary experience. Those [defending] the morality of homosexual relationships within the church may do so only by conferring upon these warrants an authority greater than the direct authority of Scripture and tradition" (210).

How Should We Respond?

The Christian community is formed by revelation rather than human delusions and confusions. Biblically, we recognize homosexual unions as contrary to God's design and ask homosexual people in our communities to remain celibate.

Since societal forces foster homosexual identity, often simple yearnings for friendship, childhood experimentation, and emotional experiences are misconstrued. One homosexual man I counseled insisted he was gay because he had "tried sex with a woman and it wasn't very satisfying." Since such an experience rips sexual union out of context, it wouldn't be satisfying for heterosexuals, either. Another counselee found her suspicions of lesbianism groundless when she rightly named her childhood experimentation. Once suspicions are planted, repeated behaviors reinforce that orientation. Instead, the Christian community must model and nurture upbuilding, nongenital same-gender friendships and thereby more positively assist young people in discovering their sexual identity according to God's creation.

Because sexual union is God's sign and gift for heterosexual marriage, any other genital activity, heterosexual or homosexual, spoils that design. Jesus' command to love requires Christian communities to welcome homosexual *persons*—but the continued call for denominations to accept homosexual *genital activity* manifests instead the persistent sexual idolatry of this age. That idolatry presently pushes many denominations toward a new hermeneutic based on a "love principle" that distorts genuine love. The Christian community, formed by God's revelation, gives primary authority to the scriptural texts and not to human experience—always remembering that those texts stand in judgment over us all.

Is It Fair?

Many respond to the biblical perspective, "That isn't fair. What gives us the right to deny homosexual persons the possibility for sexual fulfillment?"

That question displays again our sexual idolatry. It seems the Christian community is doing persons the greatest injustice ever by denying them the opportunity for sexual involvement. Why do we make sex so important? "None of the major theories asserts that the expression of genital erotic urges is essential to human well-being. Even Freudian theory, the most 'sexualized' " doesn't "posit genital gratification [as] essential to wholeness."[9]

The fairness question raises the issue of suffering. Persons addicted to sexual behavior suffer intensely to break patterns.[10] I anguish with friends who try all kinds of programs and pray earnestly for change but still find themselves sexually attracted to persons of the same gender. How can Christians be more sensitive to this acute suffering?

The crux of the matter is that we live in a broken world, filled with suffering of all sorts. Most suffering comes to us against our will, and we must decide how to respond. Homosexual persons suffer greatly because their desires do not match God's design for sexuality. They have the choice to rebel against their Creator (who is not to blame for their orientation) or to submit to his will for sexual celibacy. For the sake of God's kingdom, choosing celibacy is not too great a suffering. I don't write this blithely. Choosing celibacy was difficult for me all my single years—but possible because of the social support of the Christian community. Presently, I suffer differently—with brittle diabetes, crippled leg, deaf ear, near blindness, nerve deterioration, intestinal disorders, and now cancer. Sometimes I say that I would gladly give up sexual intercourse to see again, which shows that my idolatry now is visual rather than genital! In this broken, sinful world we all bear sufferings—physical, sexual, spiritual. Only God's grace and community support make them bearable.

How Can We Care?

The preceding analysis poses many practical questions for the Christian community.

1. How can we support homosexual persons bearing the suffering of sexual celibacy? The church serves them best by clearly maintaining—nonoppressively—its biblical, historic stance that homosexual behavior is contrary to God's design. We distin-

guish genital and social sexuality by resisting together the cultural notion that we aren't complete without genital fulfillment and by counteracting desperation for genital gratification with genuine friendship and love, the intimacies of conversation, work, and play.

2. How can we stop causing homosexual persons other kinds of suffering—by our misunderstandings, labels, failures to listen, or inability to acknowledge our complicity in sexual or other idolatrous rebellions against our Creator's designs? We are all sinners worthy of God's judgment and yet receive grace through Jesus.

How can we counteract the homophobia erupting in churches and society? How can we build friendships across the barriers between gays and straights?

3. How can we, with greater gentleness and compassion, nurse those suffering from physical illnesses or complications resulting from homosexual behavior? Besides AIDS, many medical concerns cry out for our attention.[11]

4. How can we provide better preventive medicine? Christian communities must more strongly proclaim and model God's design for human sexuality.[12] The church must thoroughly develop the awareness that, in contrast to our society's notions, human will is stronger than emotions or lusts and that we who choose the designs of God can help each other have the courage to act out of will rather than sexual desire. We can nurture gender identity by counteracting society's intimacy-shattering forces; we can display better models of deep, same-gender, nongenital friendships and provide mentoring relationships with our community's children. Together we promote God's will for personal and sexual purity and wholeness.

5. How can we help homosexual persons refrain from sexual behavior? Standing by them, we can enfold them in God's grace and love, forgive their rebellions, gently encourage their choice of God's will for their sexuality, and support them intimately with deep understanding and friendship.

Negative responses to homosexual behavior perpetuate the obsession with sexual acting out. Rather than moralistic Christianity, homosexual persons first need genuine intimacy and trust. Moreover, most homosexual behavior is already an addiction and must be treated as such. Addicted persons need recovery, not respectability.[13]

6. How can we foster change for homosexual persons? Recognizing the addictive nature of sexual behavior and the long-term struggle required to break those patterns, we must also discover the insecurities in gender identity that foster the erotic element in relationships. How can we develop the love that frees homosexual persons to relate intimately, but nonerotically, with persons of their own gender and then to develop the capacity to relate to people of the opposite sex in a healthy way, without fear or distaste?[14]

Changes from homosexuality to heterosexuality are documented, but the process is long and arduous. The Christian community must meet the profound emotional and spiritual needs of homosexual persons and offer authentic models of change. Helping them to understand the social construction of their identity and, especially, to experience God's love is basic.

7. How can we develop a vision of the kingdom of God? The Christian community must support the personhood and gifts of homosexual persons and encourage them to offer the church their insights from sacrificing genital fulfillment for the sake of larger goals in God's kingdom. As persons tempted by various idolatries, we all help each other follow Jesus in every aspect of life.

To answer precisely, we must modify the wording of our original question: Are Christianity and homosexuality incompatible? Homosexual *behavior* is not compatible with Christianity, but the church *could* be the best community in which to enfold homosexual persons in the grace of God.

NOTES

1. Stanton L. Jones, "Homosexuality According to Science," in *The Crisis of Homosexuality*, ed. J. Isamu Yamamoto (Wheaton, Ill.: Victor Books, 1990), pp. 103-14.

2. David F. Greenberg, *The Construction of Homosexuality* (Chicago: University of Chicago Press, 1988), p. 263.

3. Ibid., pp. 491, 492.

4. Required brevity here prevents establishing the whole framework in which care for homosexual persons must be understood. Please see the more thorough grounding of this chapter's ideas in Marva J. Dawn, *Sexual Character: From Technique to Intimacy* (Grand Rapids: Wm. B. Eerdmans Publishing Co., 1993), and my foundational guide for developing genuine Christian community in *The Hilarity of Community: Romans 12 and How to Be the Church* (Grand Rapids: Wm. B. Eerdmans Publishing Co., 1992).

5. For example, I agree with Maury Johnston's criticisms of the Moral Majority's unchristian attacks in *Gays Under Grace: A Gay Christian's Response to the Moral Majority* (Nashville: Winston-Derek Publishers, 1983), but his exegetical work deals falsely with texts because of his hermeneutical desires.

6. Richard B. Hays, "Relations Natural and Unnatural: A Response to John Boswell's Exegesis of Romans 1," *The Journal of Religious Ethics* 4 (Spring 1986): 184-215. Hereafter, page references to this article are given parenthetically in the text. See also my summary of Hays with expanded excursus on hermeneutical method in *Sexual Character.*

7. Ronald M. Springett, "What Does the Old Testament Say About Homosexuality?" and "What Does the New Testament Say About Homosexuality?" in *The Crisis of Homosexuality,* ed. Yamamoto, pp. 131-64.

8. Greenberg, *The Construction of Homosexuality,* pp. 199, 210-34.

9. Jones, "Homosexuality According to Science," in *The Crisis of Homosexuality,* ed. Yamamoto, p. 112.

10. Twenty-eight percent of white homosexual males report having had 1,000 or more sexual partners in a lifetime; only 17 percent report fewer than 50 partners; 79 percent report that more than half of their sexual partners were strangers. A. P. Bell and M. S. Weinberg, *Homosexualities: A Study of Diversity Among Men and Women* (New York: Simon & Schuster, 1978), p. 450.

11. Bernard J. Klamecki, "Medical Perspective of the Homosexual Issue," in *The Crisis of Homosexuality,* ed. Yamamoto, pp. 115-30.

12. Both audio and video tapes of my presentation for teens, "Godly Sexuality," are available from Christians Equipped for Ministry, 15500 N.E. Caples Rd., Brush Prairie, Washington, 98606.

13. David Neff, "Hooked on Sex," in *The Crisis of Homosexuality,* ed. Yamamoto, pp. 89-102.

14. Tim Stafford, "Coming Out," in *The Crisis of Homosexuality,* ed. Yamamoto, pp. 71-72, and Andy Comisky, *Pursuing Sexual Wholeness: How Jesus Heals the Homosexual* (Lake Mary, Fla.: Creation House, 1989).

ARE CHRISTIANITY AND HOMOSEXUALITY INCOMPATIBLE?

James B. Nelson

Chapter 4

I t is no news that matters of sexual orientation for some years now have been the most debated, the most heated, the most divisive issues in American church life. While it is typically an issue approached with fears and passions, it is also susceptible to more understanding than many realize.[1]

Many issues and questions emerge along the way, issues and questions in addition to the theological-ethical ones. But theological-ethical matters are paramount, and they engage our attention here. How shall we approach them? Protestants typically have asked, first and foremost, "What does the Bible say?" Roman Catholics typically have asked, "What does the church say?" Both questions are crucial. Neither is sufficient by itself.

One of John Wesley's legacies is the "quadrilateral" interpretation of authority, an approach with roots in Wesley's own Anglican tradition, and one still used by many persons in many communions. The quadrilateral formula reminds us that when we do our theological reflection, we must draw on more than one source. Wesley himself gave central weight to the scripture. But, over against the biblical literalizers and simplifiers, he argued that scripture must always be interpreted through the Spirit, with the indispensable aid of the church's tradition (which checks our own interpretation against the richness of past witnesses), reason (which guards against narrow and arbitrary interpretations), and experience (which is personal, inward, and enables us to interpret and appropriate the gospel).[2] Let us apply this approach to the subject of homosexuality, surely a test case for the church in our day.

Scripture

A professor of chemistry at a major university, but also by avocation a competent and published theologian, was invited to Washington, D.C., to address a large convocation of government scientists. The convention's theme was the social responsibility of science. My friend decided to open his speech in a way that would get his audience's attention but also make an important point. Here is what he said:

> I have come to Washington today with a heavy heart, for I am convinced that there are sodomites in high places in government. I am convinced that both houses of Congress have many sodomites in them, the President's cabinet is full of them, and I sadly believe that the President himself regularly practices sodomy. Now I want to tell you what sodomy is. The clearest biblical definition of this sin is not found in the Genesis story but rather in the prophet Ezekiel: "This was the guilt of your sister Sodom: she and her daughters had pride, excess of food, and prosperous ease, but did not aid the poor and needy" [Ezek. 16:49]. That, my friends, is sodomy—it is social injustice, inhospitality to the stranger.

His opening words did get the audience's attention. And he had made an important point: the real issue, whether for those scientists or for all of us, is justice. By implication, he also made another critical point: the importance of careful interpretation of scripture. The Genesis story of Sodom and Gomorrah, one of the major biblical texts used to condemn homosexuality, was centrally concerned not with sex but with the injustice of inhospitality to the stranger. To the extent that homosexual activity was condemned, it was only homosexual *rape.*[3]

Not many texts in scripture—perhaps seven at most—speak directly about homosexual behavior. We have no evidence of Jesus' teachings on or concern with the issue. The subject, obviously, is not a major scriptural preoccupation. Compare, for example, the incidence of texts on economic justice, of which there are many hundreds. In any event, what conclusions can we reach from careful assessment of the few texts in question?

My own conclusions, relying on the work of a number of contemporary biblical scholars, are several:

We receive no guidance whatsoever about the issue of sexual *orientation*. The issue of "homosexuality"—a psychosexual orientation—simply was not a biblical issue. Indeed, the concept of sexual orientation did not arise until the mid-nineteenth century. Regardless of our beliefs about the morality of same-sex expression, it is clear that our understanding of sexual *orientation* is vastly different from that of the biblical writers.

It is true, we do find condemnation of homosexual acts when they violate ancient Hebrew purity and holiness codes. We do find scriptural condemnation of homosexual prostitution. We do find condemnation of those homosexual acts which appear to be expressions of idolatry. We do find condemnation of pederasty, the sexual use of a boy by an adult male for the latter's gratification.

Note several things at this point. First, scriptural condemnation is also evident for similar *heterosexual* acts—for example, those that violate holiness codes (intercourse during menstruation), commercial sex, idolatrous heterosexual acts (temple prostitution), and the sexual misuse of minors. Further, the major questions that concern us in the present debate simply are not directly addressed in scripture. Those unaddressed issues are the theological and ethical appraisal of homosexual *orientation,* and the question of homosexual relations between adults committed to each other in mutuality and love.

Robin Scroggs concludes that "what the New Testament was against was the image of homosexuality as pederasty and primarily here its more sordid and dehumanizing dimensions. One would regret it if somebody in the New Testament had not opposed such dehumanization."[4] In short, the specific New Testament judgments against homosexual practice simply are not relevant to today's debate about the validity of caring, mutual relationships between consenting adults. Nor does the Bible directly address today's question about the appropriateness of homosexuality as a psychosexual orientation.

However, the problem concerning direct guidance from scripture about specific sexual behaviors is not unique to homosexual behaviors. The same problem arises with a host of other forms of sexual expression. The scriptures are multiform and inconsistent in the sexual moralities endorsed therein. At various points there are endorsements of sexual practices that most of us would now reject: women as the sexual property of men; the "uncleanness" of menstrual blood and semen; proscriptions against nudity within the home; the acceptance of polygamy, levirate marriage, concubinage, and prostitution.

I believe that our best biblical scholarship reaches Walter Wink's conclusion: "There is no biblical sex ethic. The Bible knows only a love ethic, which is constantly being brought to bear on whatever sexual mores are dominant in any given country, or culture, or period."[5] Even if many specific scriptural prescriptions and proscriptions regarding sex are not the gospel's word for today, there are still more basic and utterly crucial scriptural foundations for our sexual ethic.[6]

What are some of those foundations? Surely they include such affirmations as these: the created goodness of our sexuality and bodily life; the inclusiveness of Christian community, unlimited by purity codes; the equality of women and men; and the service of our sexuality to the reign of God. That incorporation of our sexuality into God's reign means expression in acts shaped by love, justice, equality, fidelity, mutual respect, compassion, and grateful joy. These are criteria that apply regardless of one's orientation. Scripture also offers ample testimony that sexual acts that degrade, demean, and harm others and ourselves are contrary to God's intent and reign. But, for more specific application of such scriptural guidance to issues of homosexuality and same-sex expression, we need to read the Scriptures in light of the other three sources.

Tradition

The postbiblical tradition provides no more unambiguous guidance on specific sexual expressions than does Scripture. Tradition most helpfully poses a series of questions—challenges to much of our conventional Christian wisdom. One question is this: Has the church's condemnation of gay and lesbian people been consistent throughout its history? As Yale historian John Boswell has demonstrated, a careful examination of tradition yields a negative answer. Indeed, for its first two centuries, the early church did not generally oppose homosexual behavior as such. Further, the opposition that did arise during the third to sixth centuries was not principally theological. Rather, it was based largely on the demise of urban culture, the increased government regulation of personal morality, and general churchly pressures toward asceticism. Following this period of opposition, however, ecclesiastical hostility to homosexuality largely disappeared once again. For some centuries there was no particular Christian antagonism toward homosexuality, and legal prohibitions were rare. Indeed, the eleventh-century urban revival saw a resurgence of gay-lesbian literature and leadership in both secular society and the church. Once again, though, hostility appeared late in the twelfth century—now as part of the general intolerance of minority groups and their presumed association with religious heresies.

Our conventional wisdom has assumed that Christian history has been all of one piece, uniform in its clear disapproval of homosexuality. In fact, a closer look at the tradition tells us that there were periods of remarkable acceptance. Further, we are reminded to interpret the theological opposition that was, indeed, often present in the context of broader changes occurring in the surrounding society.

Has the church always agreed that heterosexual marriage is

the appropriate sexual pattern? The answer is no. Singleness, particularly celibacy, was prized above marriage for much of the time from the church's beginnings to the sixteenth-century Reformation. Moreover, a careful look at tradition reveals that heterosexual marriage was not celebrated by Christian wedding services in church worship until perhaps the ninth century. We have no evidence of Christian wedding rites until that time. Obviously, many Christians married during these earlier centuries, but marriage was considered a civil order and not a rite of the church. Curiously, there is some emerging evidence that unions of gay or lesbian Christians were celebrated in some Christian churches earlier than heterosexual marriages. All of this suggests that heterosexual marriage has not always been central as the norm for Christian sexuality.

The tradition suggests a third question: Is it true that procreation has always been deemed primary to the meaning and expression of Christian sexuality? In those times wherein celibacy was more highly honored than marriage, it is obvious that procreative sex was not the norm—it was second class on the ladder of virtue. But what of the centuries, particularly since the Reformation, when marriage has been blessed as the normative Christian calling?

In the seventeenth century, a number of Christians began to teach, preach, and write about a new understanding. It appeared to them that God's fundamental purpose in creating us as sexual beings was not that we might make babies, but that we might make love. It was love, intimacy, mutuality, not procreation, that were central to the divine intention for sexuality. Most of us do not believe we must be open to procreation each time we make love—in fact, we believe strongly to the contrary. The curious double standard still exists, however; the procreative norm has been smuggled in the back door and applied negatively to lesbians and gay men.

Thus, while the church's tradition may not give definitive answers to specific questions about homosexual orientation and same-sex expression, it raises questions—these and others—that challenge conventional wisdom and refocus our perspectives.

Reason

In searching for God's truth, theologically and ethically, we need to draw on the best fruits of human reason, a third source from the quadrilateral. Wesley put it this way: "It is a fundamental principle with us that to renounce reason is to renounce religion, that religion and reason go hand in hand, and that all irrational religion is false religion."[7]

Reason is also expressed in the various sciences, our disciplined human attempts to understand creation. Biological, psychological, and social sciences can shed significant light on questions of sexual orientation. What, for example, might we learn?

In 1948 Alfred Kinsey and his associates advanced the theory that sexual orientations might be represented on a continuum. Challenging either-or assumptions (one is *either* homosexual *or* heterosexual), Kinsey introduced evidence suggesting that we might be "both/and."[8]

Though most of us tend toward one or the other side, it is probable that the vast majority of us are not exclusively either heterosexual or homosexual. Indeed, in recent decades, most sexologists have not only validated Kinsey's continuum but have also added other dimensions to it. While Kinsey was primarily interested in behaviors (genital experiences culminating in orgasm), later sexologists have argued that when other dimensions of orientation—such as fantasy, desire, social attraction, or emotional preference—are added to the picture, it is probable that none of us is exclusively one or the other. Most of us have more bisexual capacities than we have realized or than we have been taught in a bifurcating society.

Another question on which the sciences shed some light is the origin of sexual orientation. While there is still much debate, at least two things seem clear. One is that our orientations are given, not freely chosen. The likelihood is that they arise from a combination of genetic and hormonal factors, together with environmental and learning factors—both nature and nurture. The other general agreement is that our sexual orientations are established rather early in life, most likely somewhere between the ages of two and five, and thereafter are largely resistant to any dramatic changes. Some therapies may change certain behaviors, they may make some people celibate, but they will not change deep feelings and most likely will produce great psychic and emotional confusion.

Further, stereotypes about gay men and lesbians wither under scientific scrutiny. For example, the notion that homosexual males are more likely to abuse children sexually than are heterosexual males has been thoroughly disproved. Linking emotional instability or immaturity with homosexuality, likewise, is no longer scientifically tenable. Granted, lesbians and gay men suffer emotional distress from their social oppression, but this is far different from assuming that the cause of this distress lies in their orientation.

These issues do not exhaust, but simply illustrate, the ways in which the uses of human reason, including the human sciences, provide important insights for our theological reflection and understanding of scripture.

Experience

The fourth and last area of insight comes from experience. Wesley was rightly suspicious of trusting all the vagaries of human experience. Experience by itself is not reliable, nor does it give a consistent picture. However, without the validation of scriptural insight by experience as well as reason and tradition, such insight remains abstract and uncompelling. The Spirit, Wesley believed, inwardly validates God's truth through our experience.

I lived the first forty years of my life without carefully looking at my own feelings about sexual orientations. Then, about 1970 through some volunteer work in urban ministries, I came into close contact—for the first time that I consciously recognized—with a number of articulate gay men and lesbians who challenged my stereotypes and launched me into an examination of my own homophobia.

Though my genital experience had been completely heterosexual, I now discovered that I was not "completely heterosexual" but only dominantly so. I was capable of occasional same-sex feelings, too, though society had taught me to deny them and blame others (gays and lesbians) for having what I had a bit of as well. In addition, I learned that I had resented gay males who broke the masculinity stereotypes and seemed to threaten my own commitment to culturally defined masculinity. I also had resented lesbians, for they were living proof that at least some women did not need men to complete them as persons. Further, I recognized my fear of gay males who might "womanize" me by treating me as a passive sexual object, which was precisely the way society had taught men to view women. I also recognized that in looking at gays through social stereotypes I saw them as very sexual people, and that made me secretly envious. It confused me as well, for my culture had taught me that "real men" were always ready for sex, and by appearing so sexual gay men seemed more "manly" than I. In addition, I envied the male bonding I saw among gays—an emotional intimacy that I seldom had with other men. Furthermore, both gay men and lesbians made me anxious about death, for they were symbols of nonprocreating people in a society where children seem to protect us from our death fears.

When experience is carefully examined, it can be an important source of theological insight. These are some of the dynamics of homophobia I recognized in my own experience years ago. In sum, I learned that my homophobia was really fear of myself. But the gospel has resources for dealing with fear.[9]

The basic issue is not homosexuality but rather *human* sexuality. Our sexuality, I believe, is a precious gift from God, critically important as part of a divine invitation. It is an invitation that we come together with each other and with God in relationships of intimacy and celebration, of faithfulness and tenderness, of love and justice. Our sexuality is a gift to be integrated fully and joyously into our spirituality. Our orientations, whatever they may be, are part of that gift—to be received with thanksgiving and honored by each other.[10]

NOTES

1. This chapter is abridged with author's and publisher's permission from chapter 4, "Sources for Body Theology: Homosexuality as a Test Case," in James B. Nelson, *Body Theology* (Louisville: Ky.: Westminster/John Knox Press, 1992).

2. An excellent discussion of Wesley's quadrilateral can be found in Colin W. Williams, *John Wesley's Theology Today* (Nashville: Abingdon Press, 1960), chap. 2.

3. For more detail about the specific biblical texts that make direct references to certain forms of same-sex activity, see James B. Nelson, *Embodiment: An Approach to Sexuality and Christian Theology* (Minneapolis: Augsburg Publishing House, 1978), chap. 3 no. 7, and chap. 8.

4. Robin Scroggs, *The New Testament and Homosexuality* (Philadelphia: Fortress Press, 1983), p. 126.

5. Walter Wink, "Biblical Perspectives on Homosexuality," *The Christian Century*, Dec. 7, 1979, p. 1085.

6. L. William Countryman, *Dirt, Greed, and Sex* (Philadelphia: Fortress Press, 1988).

7. John Wesley, in *The Letters of John Wesley*, ed. John Telford, standard ed., vol. 5 (London: Epworth Press, 1931), p. 364. Commenting on 1 Corinthians 14:20, Wesley also said, "Knowing religion was not designed to destroy any of our natural faculties, but to exalt and improve them, our reason in particular." Cf. Williams, *John Wesley's Theology Today*, p. 30.

8. See Alfred C. Kinsey et al., *Sexual Behavior in the Human Male* (Philadelphia: W. B. Saunders, 1948). See also his *Sexual Behavior in the Human Female* (Philadelphia: W. B. Saunders, 1953).

9. For a fuller discussion of the dynamics of homophobia, see James B. Nelson, *The Intimate Connection: Male Sexuality, Masculine Spirituality* (Philadelphia: Westminster Press, 1988), chap. 3, no. 3, and pp. 59ff.

10. For a review of literature on the subject of this chapter, see my article "Homosexuality and the Church: A Bibliographical Essay," *Prism* 6 (Spring 1991): 74-83.

STUDY GUIDE

In recent years many denominational bodies have reaffirmed policies stating that the practice of homosexuality is incompatible with Christian teaching. A basic assumption of these pronouncements rests on the assumption characterizing homosexual behavior as sinful.

Marva J. Dawn upholds these historic church stands, while

James B. Nelson sets forth on the basis of Scripture, tradition, reason, and experience why he thinks these policies are erroneous. Dawn speaks of the idolatry of sex for both heterosexual and homosexual persons, urging celibacy and upholding suffering as a Christian virtue. Nelson emphasizes a body theology that affirms sexuality as God's good creation, contending Christians should not repress gay and lesbian expressions of love.

Items for Reflection

1. Is homosexuality a sin? If you believe it is, do you think it is more or less serious than other sins listed in the Bible? Why?

2. Does the cause of homosexual orientation significantly influence your viewpoint on whether Christianity and homosexuality are compatible?

3. Should gays and lesbians be denied certain occupations in society? Should they have the equal right to serve in the military of their country? Why or why not?

4. How do you understand the meaning of suffering? Or idolatry?

SUGGESTED RESOURCES

Dawn, Marva, *Sexual Character: From Technique to Intimacy*. Grand Rapids: Wm. B. Eerdmans Publishing Co., 1993.

Hasbany Richard, ed. *Homosexuality and Religion*. New York and London: Harrington Park Press, 1989. Articles from ecumenical sources, Catholic, Protestant, and Jew.

Mickey, Paul A. *Of Sacred Worth*. Nashville: Abingdon Press, 1991. Argues that gays and lesbians are persons of sacred worth, but homosexual practices are incompatible with Christian faith.

Nelson, James B. *Body Theology*. Louisville, Ky.: Westminster/John Knox Press, 1992.

CHAPTER 5

SHOULD GAYS AND LESBIANS BE ORDAINED?

Richard C. Looney

Chapter 5

The ordination of practicing homosexual persons is forbidden by the overwhelming majority of Christian denominations. While the debate continues to be intense, there remains a strong consensus that the practice of homosexuality is contrary to God's intention. My denomination affirms that "self-avowed practicing homosexuals are not to be accepted as candidates, ordained as ministers, or appointed to serve in the church." This position is a logical outgrowth of the church's teaching on human sexuality. While sexuality is a good gift of a loving God, "sexual relations are only clearly affirmed in the marriage bond." Marriage is "expressed in love, mutual support, personal commitment, and shared fidelity between a man and a woman."[1]

Since this wonderful, mysterious gift of God is to be expressed and protected only within the bond of marriage between a man and a woman, any expression outside that relationship is incompatible with Christian teaching. Such incompatible practices would include sexual relations between family members (incest), sexual relations with animals (bestiality), sexual relations before marriage (fornication), sexual relations outside marriage (adultery), and sexual relations between persons of the same sex (homosexuality).

The vast majority of Christians through the centuries have affirmed that the church does not condone the practice of homosexuality and considers this practice incompatible with Christian teaching. Therefore, those who are set apart for ordained ministry are "required to maintain the highest standards represented by the practice of fidelity in marriage and celibacy in singleness."[2]

To ordain persons who choose to profess and practice a life-style that the church does not condone would be both confusing and destructive. The church has the right and responsibility to specify what behavior is appropriate for persons it sets apart for ordained ministry, based on its understanding of Scripture, tradition, reason, and experience.

This classical Christian position is now being questioned, and too often in intimidating language that does little to enhance understanding. The church's position on homosexuality is an expression of its conviction concerning God's will for the human family. Yet those who hold the traditional position are often labeled homophobic, uninformed, reactionary, or even hateful. Surely the discussion of this complex issue deserves a more rational and understanding treatment. To dismiss carelessly the testimony of Paul and Augustine; or Martin Luther, John Calvin, and Karl Barth;[3] or the many sincere believers who have struggled with this issue serves no one well. If the church were to decide to ordain "self-avowed practicing homosexuals," it would be required to affirm that the practice of homosexuality *is* compatible with Christian teaching and that marriage should be approved between persons of the same sex.

To propose such a radical reversal would require the church to either ignore or explain away the consistent witness of Scripture, make a dramatic break with Judeo-Christian tradition, overlook a high-risk and unnatural violation of the human anatomy, affront the moral conviction of most of its members, radically redefine the institution of marriage, and dramatically reinterpret the meaning of ordination.

Conviction with Compassion

It is important to note that the church seeks to balance very carefully its conviction with compassion. My church's teaching insists that

> all persons, regardless of age, gender, marital status, or sexual orientation, are entitled to have their human and civil rights ensured. . . . Homosexual persons no less than heterosexual persons are individuals of sacred worth. . . . We affirm that God's grace is available to all.[4]

Here is a blending of compassion for persons and conviction concerning conduct. Although all persons are of sacred worth, not all practices are compatible with Christian teaching. It is possible to love persons while disapproving their behavior. A careful reading of the social principles and resolutions of many mainline denominations will reveal many practices that are not condoned.[5] In those cases, the church is not accused of being unloving, hateful, phobic, or literalistic.

A beautiful illustration of the blending of compassion and conviction was demonstrated by a sensitive mother in south Georgia. She had cared lovingly for her son who was dying of AIDS. She wrote the following:

> The challenge was to love him in such a way that even though we thought his behavior to be sin, he would never think we rejected him because of it. It occurs to me that the church is now in much the same position that we were as parents. Intense pressure to compromise is being brought to bear. But I believe compromise on the issue will not result in the redemption of souls. And the challenge for the church will be, as it was for us, how to love them in such a way that they know of our love, in spite of our unwillingness to condone their sin.[6]

Orientation and Behavior

It is also important to note the distinction made between orientation and behavior. There are tendencies in all of us that are to be resisted, not affirmed or followed. A predisposition toward certain thought or action does not mean it is a good gift or morally correct. Many persons are predisposed to promiscuity, immaturity, gambling, alcoholism, or a long list of other temptations. The Christian faith offers not only the motivation but the divine power to resist what is contrary to God's intention for human behavior.

In all of us there are flaws to be forgiven and overcome. Whether that flaw can be traced to nature or nurture, it is sin for which God in Christ provides forgiveness and the ability to overcome. No one is barred from the ministry because of predisposition or tendency. But persons who choose to practice what the church does not condone disqualify themselves.

With these clarifications, let us now move to a fuller treatment of the church's traditional position and review the rationale for its continuance. It is crucial to understand that the church has the responsibility to set standards for persons it sets aside for ordained ministry. The standards are based on reasons that are *scriptural, historical, rational,* and *loving.*

Scripture

For most Christians, Scripture is always primary. Earlier contributors to this book have discussed the biblical material, but it is crucial to understand the force of its witness. By repeated statements, positive and negative, it is clear that sexual relations are to be expressed within the bonds of marriage between a man and a woman. Beginning with Genesis and continuing through the Old and New Testaments, the mystery of man and woman becoming "one flesh" is celebrated.

The practice of homosexuality is forbidden without exception and in strong language. There is not even a hint that such practice should be condoned or encouraged. In Leviticus 18:22 and 20:13, the practice of homosexuality is called "an abomination." In Romans 1:26-27, Paul speaks of "degrading passions," "unnatural" and "shameless acts." In 1 Corinthians 6:9-10, homosexual acts along with fornication, idolatry, greed, and drunkenness prohibit one from entering the Kingdom. In 1 Timothy 1:8-11, sodomy and fornication are included among other acts that are "contrary to the sound teaching."

While all of us must guard against the danger of using the Scriptures for our own needs (proof-texting), the witness is consistent and clear. We are not embarrassed to condemn in strong terms the other practices included in these lists with homosexual practice. On what basis do we carefully extract one but leave the others?

The strong feelings around the issue of homosexuality are sometimes intensified by the way some proponents of ordination for practicing homosexual persons handle the scriptural material. In an attempt to explain away or reinterpret, they imply that the biblical witness can be easily set aside or discredited. Without an anchor in revealed religion or historical faith, the church is at the mercy of every new fad or social movement. One position becomes as valid as any other. The church will then be swayed by those who can argue or lobby the most persuasively. Persons ordained for ministry are expected to uphold the scriptural witness.

Traditional and Global Understanding

The church's present understanding of Scripture is illumined by tradition. The current statements on the practice of homosexuality are overwhelmingly confirmed in Jewish and Christian teaching. Although tradition is never elevated to a place of infallibility, "Christianity does not leap from the New Testament times to the present as though nothing were to be learned from that great cloud of witnesses in between."[7] Those ordained for ministry are to "maintain fidelity to the apostolic faith."[8]

The early church fathers, such as Augustine, Chrysostom, and Aquinas; the reformers, such as Martin Luther and John Calvin; and such twentieth-century theologians as Karl Barth used language as strong as the biblical writers in condemning homosexual practice. These include phrases such as "shameful act against nature," "insult to nature," "injury to creation," "fearful crime of unnatural lust," and "distortion of God's norm."[9] To set aside such a consistent consensus would create shattering confusion in the Christian community.

The conviction that homosexual practice is incompatible with Christian teaching is also consistent with the general view of world Christianity. I have been privileged to participate in short-term mission trips to Africa, Central America, and Latin America, and I have visited churches in Singapore and Malaysia. Time after time church leaders express amazement that the church in the United States could be spending so much energy on a matter that is clearly forbidden in Scripture and classical Christianity. To choose to ordain practicing homosexual persons would move us outside the boundaries of a global church.

Medical Science

The church's position on homosexual practice is also informed by the findings of medical science. For example, evidence suggests that anal sex, as frequently practiced by many homosexual men and increasingly by some heterosexual couples, is a violation of the human anatomy. This practice places the receptive partner at high risk for a wide range of sexually transmitted and other exotic diseases. The studies are voluminous, easily accessible in medical libraries, and generally ignored. There is almost a conspiracy of silence around this issue.

Admittedly, it is indelicate to talk about anal sex. It seems crude to discuss a delicate tract created to hold and expel waste being used in an unnatural way for sexual pleasure. But love for persons does not ignore unpleasant realities. To affirm high-risk behavior as an alternative life-style may be cruel rather than compassionate.

Through a computer search, I was made aware of more than one hundred articles on male homosexuality and the dangers of anal intercourse. In reading more than three dozen of these reports, I discovered a convincing corollary to the biblical description of this practice as unnatural. The anal canal is very fragile and easily torn, providing a ready entry point for AIDS and other sexually transmitted diseases—parasitic diseases, hepatitis A and B viruses, and others. A careful examination of the intended function of the human anatomy, the requirements of basic hygiene, and the medical consequences of certain behavior convinces me that the church is acting out of love and with reason in its position on homosexual practice.

Those who take the church's traditional position are often depicted as persons with heads in the sand (or past) who will be bypassed by the enlightenment now available in the scientific community. But that community does not speak with one voice, and the scientific facts seem to change with regularity. For instance, it has been assumed almost as a given that homosexual males make up 10 percent of the general population. But studies released in April 1993 set the percentage between 1.1 percent and 2.3 percent.[10]

Other assumptions, upon examination, prove to carry a divided opinion. There continues to be a respected minority of psychiatrists who strongly oppose the American Psychiatric Association's vote in 1973 to remove homosexuality from its list of pathological adaptations. In their letter condemning the recent vote by the American Psychoanalytic Association to accept openly homosexual persons as trainees within the Psychoanalytic Institute, cochairmen of the group organized as the Committee of Concerned Psychoanalysts said:

> If a diagnosis of homosexuality is going to be deleted by the American Psychoanalytic Association, as it was by the American Psychiatric Association, let us be clear. We believe that what would be decided now would have far reaching consequences regarding . . . the freedom of psychiatrists to help patients who had come to them because they were not satisfied with their homosexuality and did not believe that they were born homosexual.[11]

Numerous genetic and hormonal theories have surfaced that have not subsequently proven definitive. Human behavior is a very complex matter to diagnose. To imply that the scientific community is of one mind is presumptuous, if not dishonest.

A Hopeful Position

The church's position is also hopeful for it dares to say, "It is possible to change or withstand inclinations that are counter to God's will for human behavior." In trying to understand other persons' struggles, we do not honor them by implying that they have no control over their behavior. Determinism is a demeaning doctrine in every age.

There is significant support in the scientific community for the belief that practice and orientation can be changed when strong motivation is joined with therapy and loving support. Some therapists declare that no such change is possible, but other respected therapists report noteworthy success rates.[12]

Such hope is illustrated in a letter I received in 1992:

> Breaking free from a homosexual orientation has been the biggest struggle of my life, but one which has been well worth the effort. A Christian counselor helped pinpoint the problem and uncovered a volcano of erupting emotions. At age 25, I broke free from the bonds of homosexuality and began to experience heterosexual feelings. As you know, I am now a happily married man with beautiful children. I am convinced that motivation is the single most important factor. Persons who are convinced that homosexual practice is against God's will for their lives can find the motivation to be set free. I am glad that I didn't get shortchanged.[13]

The letter closes with these words: "I'm writing you because I am convinced that our church's teaching will have a critical bearing on the decisions made by homosexuals who are struggling to find God's will for their lives. I encourage you to maintain the firm, compassionate stance [of the church]."[14] Those who represent the church affirm the possibility of transformation for those who desire it.

The Church's Responsibility to Affirm Standards

Finally, the church has the right and responsibility to affirm standards of appropriate sexual conduct for members and ordained ministers. Persons are free to choose whatever standard they wish, but the church cannot be expected to bless what it considers contrary to Scripture, tradition, reason, or experience. This is especially true for those the church sets apart for ordained ministry. Such persons are expected to be faithful in interpreting and practicing the biblical message and apostolic faith.

From New Testament times, the church set forth specific qualifications for its leaders. Any call to ministry was to be confirmed and validated by the church. There were high expectations concerning abilities and behavior. Dennis M. Campbell, dean of Duke Divinity School, has observed:

> These leaders were to articulate the gospel of Jesus Christ, to teach the faith, to help others practice the faith in daily life, and to be exemplars of the faith representing Christ to church and world. . . . Ordination had to do chiefly with authenticity in assuring the apostolic character of Christian faith. It was essential that these "holy mysteries" be administered by one who was "under orders," and "officially" obedient to the community, so that the people could be certain that they were served by a faithful shepherd.[15]

To represent the church, one must submit individual inclinations to the will of the body. The right of ordination is bestowed by the church on those it has examined and affirmed. Theological and biblical understanding, moral behavior, relational skills, and any number of other attributes are taken into account. Personal desires are subordinated to the teaching and expectations of the church. As Dennis M. Campbell has noted, "The question is whether the candidate will abide by and teach what the church determines to be its understanding of responsible practice of human sexuality."[16] For United Methodists, that means either "fidelity in marriage" or "celibacy in singleness."[17] With rare exception, this remains the prevailing normative standard of sexuality for almost all Christian denominations.

In conclusion, the church disapproves of homosexual practice, but its members can never allow themselves to despise or dehumanize persons who engage in such practice. "Love is what the church has generally failed to show to homosexual persons," says John Stott, but instead has treated them as "objects of scorn and insult, of fear, prejudice and oppression."[18] Stott reminds us that "love is concerned for the highest welfare of the beloved, and our highest human welfare is found in obedience to God's law and purpose."[19] That purpose is never dictated by the mood of contemporary culture, but by the church's understanding of God's revealed will through Scripture, enlightened by tradition, reason, and experience.

NOTES

1. *The Book of Discipline of The United Methodist Church* (Nashville: The United Methodist Publishing House, 1992), par 402, p. 202; par. 71, pp. 91, 90. Though I cite from United Methodist documents, I could produce parallel statements from other denominations.

2. Ibid., par. 402, p. 202; par. 71, p. 92.

3. See Karl Barth, *Church Dogmatics, 3/4* (Edinburgh: T & T Clark, 1961), esp. p. 166. See also excerpt from Karl Barth, "Church Dogmatics," in *Homosexuality and Ethics*, ed. Edward Batchelor, Jr. (New York: Pilgrim Press, 1980), pp. 48-51.

4. *Discipline*, par. 71, pp. 91, 92.

5. For a comprehensive collection of official church resources specifically on homosexuality, see J. Gordon Melton, ed. *The Churches Speak on Homosexuality: Official Statements from Religious Bodies and Ecumenical Organizations* (Detroit: Gale Research, 1991).

6. Personal letter, Dec. 3, 1991, used with permission.

7. *Discipline*, par. 68, p. 79.

8. Ibid., par. 68, p. 80.

9. Richard F. Lovelace, *Homosexuality and the Church* (Old Tappan, N.J.: Fleming H. Revell Co., 1978), pp. 17-24.

10. *U.S. News and World Report*, April 26, 1993, pp. 22-23; *Newsweek*, April 26, 1993, pp. 55-57.

11. Charles W. Socaradies, M.D., and C. Downing Tait, M.D., cochairmen, Committee of Concerned Psychoanalysts, Letters to the Editor, *The American Psychoanalyst* 27 (1993).

12. Roger J. Magnuson, *Are Gay Rights Right?* (Portland, Oreg.: Multnomah Press, 1990), p. 59. See also John Stott, *Involvement*, vol. 2 (Old Tappan, N.J.: Fleming H. Revell Co., 1984), pp. 239-42.

13. Personal letter, March 29, 1992, used with permission.

14. Ibid.

15. Dennis M. Campbell, *The Yoke of Obedience* (Nashville: Abingdon Press, 1988), pp. 28, 32.

16. Ibid., p. 93.

17. *Discipline,* par. 402, p. 202.

18. *Involvement,* p. 242.

19. Ibid., p. 235.

SHOULD GAYS AND LESBIANS BE ORDAINED?

Tex S. Sample

Chapter 5

ave had strong attachments to boys even before he was a teenager. By the time he was fifteen, he felt "different." Although he dated several girls from junior high through high school, he simply "knew" that somehow he did not have the kind of feelings the other boys had toward girls. A careful student, he received above average marks from his teachers, and as a high school basketball player good enough to be popular, he was well accepted by other students. Yet, he grew increasingly uncomfortable with his powerful attraction to other boys. Active in his local church, he began in his junior year to have a very troublesome urge to go into the ministry.

Letting no one know of either his increasingly clear same-sex attractions or his sense of urgency about the ministry, Dave entered college as an English major. Toward the end of his sophomore year, he met and eventually fell in love with John. Within six months they were giving intimate sexual expression to their relationship, which only deepened Dave's dilemma about his sexual orientation and call to the ministry. At that point he began a concentrated study of homosexuality, and out of his deepening love for John, he moved toward an acceptance of his sexual identity, a move significantly helped by a college chaplain who believed, though straight himself, that such orientations were a gift from God to be claimed and celebrated.

Upon learning of Dave's call to the ministry, the chaplain encouraged him to move toward seminary, a decision decidedly supported by John but one filled with anxiety. During Dave's and John's senior year, the chaplain conducted a holy union between them, and that fall Dave entered a theological school in the Midwest. In seminary, Dave was a solid student and grew enormously in his love of the ministry and the church, but his concern mounted as he struggled to decide whether he would shift his membership to the Metropolitan Community Church or become a Unitarian Universalist, two denominations that accept gays and lesbians for ordination. Dave's love for his denomination pushed him to want to try to stay in it, but he also loved John more than ever, and celibacy was not a relevant consideration.

Presently, Dave's denomination will not ordain self-avowed practicing homosexual persons. It does not matter whether such persons sense a deep call or live in faithful unions as do Dave and John or demonstrate gifts and graces for ordained ministry as Dave clearly does. Should this denomination change its position? I say yes. The question is, On what grounds?[1]

The Kingdom of God

The kingdom of God is the righteous rule of God. In the New Testament, Jesus inaugurates this realm with his coming and becomes the hope of the world in his promised coming again. In the Gospel of Luke (4:18-21), Jesus announces his ministry in the passage from Isaiah (61:1-2*a*) "to bring good news to the poor," "to proclaim release to the captives," "recovery of sight to the blind,/to let the oppressed go free,/to proclaim the year of the Lord's favor." He then states, "Today this scripture has been fulfilled in your hearing" (v. 21). His ministry is clearly one of both redemption and liberation. Indeed, his very presence represents this reign.[2]

The story of this Kingdom—and our call to serve it—is the

epitome of everything for which the church lives and gives its life. Any question, therefore, before the church must finally be raised in terms of its relationship to God's rule. It is, if you will, the final court of appeal for any matter before the church.

The kingdom of God becomes monumentally crucial on the question of the ordination of homosexual persons because no other questions seem relevant until this is addressed. For example, a number of denominations would ordain Dave on the basis of his baptism, his academic record, his deep sense of call, his moral character (except for his altogether faithful union with John), his clear gifts and graces for ministry, and his love for the church and active participation in it over the years. He is a fine candidate except for his life with John, as things presently stand.

Moreover, anyone who knows the church well knows gay and lesbian persons who have served the church with enormous distinction as clergy, although their homosexual orientation and practice are not known. In my experience, the church would be impoverished by their absence, and people served by them would testify overwhelmingly to the authenticity of their call, the effectiveness of their work, the manifestation of the gospel through them, and their capacity to equip the saints through their ministry. Such persons meet all appropriate standards for ordination except for their homosexual practices. The issue thus comes down to the question of whether some homosexual practices manifest and serve the kingdom of God.

Scripture, Tradition, and Homosexuality

Doubtless, it seems strange that I should make faithfulness to the kingdom of God the basic criterion for the ordination of homosexual persons since some translations of Scripture explicitly state that persons who engage in same-sex acts cannot inherit the Kingdom (1 Cor. 6:9, 1 Tim. 1:10). Attention to these passages will be given in other chapters in this book, but let me state as straightforwardly as I can the basic issue here. These passages are directed against male cultic prostitution, specifically the exploitative use of young boys by older men. Such practices are ruled out of the kingdom of God, and the church ought not to ordain persons engaged in such practices. Neither should it ordain heterosexuals involved in activities that exploit the young in *opposite-sex* encounters. But this teaching has nothing to do with a relationship like that of Dave and John. These are two fine young Christian men who love each other.

The other key New Testament text on this issue is Romans 1:24-27. It is quite clear that Paul's teaching here is about certain same-sex acts of his day, and his view is one widely held in the ancient world, for which we have evidence in numerous texts from that time. The view maintained that people who had grown jaded and tired of their promiscuous opposite-sex debauches in their boredom turned to same-sex activities to stimulate their deadened erotic lives. In Paul's view, the same-sex practices did not cause the rupture between God and human beings. Rather, human idolatry that led to God's wrath and judgment on the world "gave them up to degrading passions" (v. 26). For Paul, same-sex practices were one consequence of God's judgment on human idolatry. Paul contended that everyone was guilty of idolatry, although not all had practiced same-sex acts. Hence, all had sinned and were unrighteous (Rom. 3:22-23).[3]

What must be understood is that the same-sex practices Paul describes are decidedly not the kind of homosexual practices under consideration here. To condemn same-sex practices across the board is to go beyond the teaching of this passage and to bring an agenda to Scripture from outside the text.

In the case of Dave and John, they did not grow tired of promiscuous heterosexual activity and turn to same-sex acts to seek relief from a sensual and existential boredom. Neither of them has had *any* sexual intimacies with women. Both report that as they became aware of their sexuality, they increasingly knew they were attracted to persons of the same gender. It was a growing consciousness of what had always been so but had not been adequately named and acknowledged. Such a development is not addressed by Paul or by anyone else in the Bible.

The World of Scripture, the Contemporary World, and Experience

The Scriptures reveal everything that is necessary for our salvation. However, on some questions we have knowledge available to us that they did not. One clear example is the biblical view of the three-story universe (the heaven above, the flat earth, and the chaotic waters beneath the earth [Exod. 20:4]). This view of the world is assumed or explicitly used throughout the Bible; even the teachings of Jesus reflect it. Our view of the universe following Galileo, Newton, Einstein, and others was not available to the people of biblical times.

This is one reason why we need the resource of experience in theological method. If we could quote the Scriptures on any issue where there was even an oblique reference related to a contemporary matter, we would not need experience to understand biblical teaching. We cannot be content to quote texts that speak to specific and clearly violative same-sex practices and then characterize all homosexual relations the same way, especially those constituted of fidelity and commitment like that of Dave and John.

But what about tradition? There is no question that the weight of tradition has been opposed to same-sex practices. Exceptions to this can be found; nevertheless, the dominant picture is negative. What is also clear is how much this negative judgment is shaped by a misunderstanding of the teaching of Scripture and by these same limited views of the ancient world.

A New Basis in Scripture and Tradition

Do the limitations on Scripture and tradition mean that we can find no help in them for dealing with this issue? No, not if we raise the question, as indicated above, in terms of the kingdom of God. Most churches are prepared to ordain homosexual persons who remain celibate, especially if they remain silent about their sexuality. Thus, the focus of this section is on lesbians and gays who are in unions. Three basic issues relate to clear teachings on the kingdom of God.

The first of these concerns erotic passion and its relationship to God's kingdom. It is interesting that Paul, even though he believed the Kingdom was coming soon and favored the practice of celibacy, nevertheless was sensitive to erotic passion. He did not suggest that all simply be celibate, as he himself apparently was (1 Cor. 7:8-9). When same-sex orientation is understood as a given in the lives of homosexual persons, it seems strange to believe that it is better to be "aflame with passion." To rephrase Paul, it is better for Dave and John to form a union than to burn with desire.[4]

Some, of course, argue that ex-gays have overcome their orientation and have been transformed out of such passion. While this position assumes that homosexual orientation is wrong, and I do not, I have no interest in denying the experience of people who are obviously sincere. It is clear, however, that this is a possibility for some, not all, and that it is probably true of a highly specialized population at that. After more than forty years of research on gender identity and sexual orientation, John Money, director of the Psychohormonal Research Unit of the Johns Hopkins University School of Medicine, has observed that "it is no more possible to change a homosexual orientation into a heterosexual one than it is—take special note!—to change a heterosexual orientation into a homosexual one." He reports that claims of change in orientations when carefully examined turn out to be those of "persons who are bisexual to some degree (e.g., 80:20, 40:60, or even 50:50), but are not 100% homosexual, nor 100% heterosexual."[5] Nevertheless, it is not enough to argue that people need to meet their sexual desires. The issue must move on to that of their relation to the kingdom of God.

Second, I am interested in the figurative use of marriage in the Hebrew scriptures to express the covenantal relation between God and the people of Israel both in faithfulness (Jer. 2:2) and in unfaithfulness (Hos. 2:2, 19-20). In the New Testament, marriage is used to express the relationship between Christ and the church (2 Cor. 11:2; Eph. 5:23; Rev. 19:7-9). Both suggest a profound analogy between fidelity in marriage and the faithfulness of the people of God, a fidelity characteristic of the kingdom of God.

That fidelity in marriage is such a key figurative way to understand the relation between God and Israel and between Christ and the church opens up powerful perspectives on gay and lesbian unions that witness to the same depths of commitment and caring. Dave and John have been in love for five years and in a faithful union for four. By being up-front about their relationship, they have from time to time experienced enormous social disapproval. On one occasion John was severely beaten by three young men shouting, "Death to queers!" Although Dave's mother and father have come to accept his homosexuality and to love John, none of the extended family will have anything to do with them, and one uncle insists on calling them "perverts."

They cope with things like this all the time, yet they remain faithful to the church and to each other. This kind of tormented struggle bespeaks the human face of fidelity in which we see signs of God's steadfast love. A question of this magnitude does not revolve around the gender makeup of the two persons but the dedicated character of their relationship to each other and to God.

Finally, an interesting turn occurs in the New Testament in the relativizing of marriage and family—and all other institutions, for that matter—when it comes to the kingdom of God. Jesus clearly states that "whoever does the will of God is my brother and sister and mother" (Mark 3:35). Hence, family is redefined as those who are committed to the Kingdom. Teaching like this requires an entirely new way of looking at a relationship like that of Dave and John. The question of their union—and celibacy and marriage as well, for that matter—is whether it serves the kingdom of God.

Three Fundamental Questions

In the light of this discussion, three fundamental questions must be asked of a union like theirs to ascertain whether further consideration can be given for ordination for someone like Dave.

The first is whether one's union basically frustrates one's commitment to the kingdom of God. There is no question that some unions can be an occasion for compulsive, obsessive, exploitative, or oppressive behavior that defies the evangelical message of God's good news in Jesus. Like celibacy or marriage, a union can stifle a stand for justice or peace. It can be an unholy deadlock that consumes one in trivia and a deflected existence. When such occurs, and these are obviously not exhaustive, one's relationship becomes a hindrance to ministry and cannot be justified. But this is simply not the case with Dave and John.

The second issue for ordination is whether one's union, like marriage or celibacy, frees one for obedience to God and propels one to fulfill God's aims. True freedom in Christian life is found in a fully orbed obedience to God, to live out the life God intends. There is no question that some unions, as some marriages, free people to live life more fully in the Spirit. The strengths of each partner redound to the gifts and graces of the other, and a life in mission results. So the issue becomes one of whether one's relationship nurtures and enhances one's commitment to others, one's service to the church, and one's steadfastness to the realm of God. Here, again, Dave would tell you how supportive John has been of his call to ministry and how John has stayed with him as he encountered frustrating barricades and detours.

Finally, and perhaps most important, does the union itself bear witness to the covenantal reality of the kingdom of God? I think here particularly of fidelity as a key virtue of the Kingdom, as a practice that is intrinsic to the righteousness of God. In other words, if covenant is basic to God's rule, does one's union manifest a basic dimension of covenantal life together? With Dave and John and dozens of other people that I know in unions, I say yes.

These, then, are the key issues to be addressed in the ordination of Dave or, for that matter, anyone else. But let it be clear that I am no more suggesting that the church approve all homosexual behaviors than I am heterosexual ones. Promiscuity, whatever the orientation, makes one unready for ordination. To be sure, unfaithful practices exist besides promiscuity. Self-avowed bigotry in racism, sexism, or classism makes one as unready as self-avowed promiscuity.

In conclusion, the church faces new questions with respect to the ordination of homosexual persons. Neither Scripture nor tradition faces the consideration before us today. On the issue of homosexuality and ordination we are more authoritatively informed by the New Testament view on the kingdom of God. Careful attention to this teaching raises far more significant criteria for the ordination of persons to ministry in the church. When homosexual unions are faithful to God's rule, manifest its power, serve its aims, and bespeak its hopes and joys, the basic question of readiness for ordained ministry has been met.

NOTES

1. The reason for the heavier focus of this paper on gay men is that resistance in the church seems so much greater to them than to lesbians, although I do not wish to minimize the opposition to ordination of the latter or to women in ministry in general.

Moreover, my true story of Dave and John chooses a gay couple with few "complications." Not all homosexual persons seeking ordination are like them, but neither are all heterosexuals without "complicated" histories. The issue of faithfulness to the kingdom of God gives us a way to deal with people as forgiven but raises hard questions about their readiness for ordained ministry. I am not arguing a moral relativism or that we should just accept people—whatever the orientation—with the kind of inane, unaccountable cheap grace that traipses around the church. Grace is given not to accommodate us to the world but so that we can be transformed for the Kingdom.

2. For discussions that take the kingdom of God with the utmost seriousness, see John Howard Yoder, *The Politics of Jesus* (Grand Rapids: Wm. B. Eerdmans Publishing Co., 1972), and Stanley J. Hauerwas, *The Peaceable Kingdom* (Notre Dame: University of Notre Dame Press, 1983). For a contrasting but important perspective on the commonwealth of God, see Beverly Harrison, *Making the Connections* (Boston: Beacon Press, 1985), esp. pp. 135-51.

3. See Robin Scroggs, *The New Testament and Homosexuality: Contextual Background for Contemporary Debate* (Philadelphia: Fortress Press, 1983),

and Victor Paul Furnish, *The Moral Teaching of Paul: Selected Issues*, rev. ed. (Nashville: Abingdon Press, 1985), pp. 52-82.

4. Questions inevitably arise about homosexual practices, although these practices do not involve anything heterosexuals do not do—oral-genital sex, anal intercourse, etc.—except that they are same-sex. For example, studies reveal that about 20 percent of heterosexuals engage in anal intercourse, which in sheer numbers of persons makes it a much larger heterosexual than homosexual practice. This does not necessarily make it right—which is another matter in itself—but why has this question not been raised with heterosexuals who seek ordination?

Some argue that same-sex acts are unnatural. We now know how "nature" is used and has been used ideologically to defend a status quo against marginalized persons. See Raymond Williams, *Problems in Materialism and Culture* (London: Verso, 1980), pp. 67-85. Hardly any claim is as unreliable as an argument from "nature."

5. Correspondence, Oct. 1, 1991.

STUDY GUIDE

Self-avowed practicing homosexual persons often are prohibited by church law from being ordained or serving as clergypersons in most denominations. The biblical and ecclesiastical rationales for this restriction are articulated, along with the arguments used to challenge this position.

Bishop Richard Looney justifies excluding gays and lesbians from ordination by emphasizing biblical prohibitions against homosexual behavior and by accenting the long tradition of many denominations explicitly forbidding homosexual persons from being ordained. Tex Sample challenges this thinking by arguing that gays and lesbians, living in faithful covenantal relationships or unions with a partner, can have the qualities of spirit and competence as required in the kingdom of God.

Items for Reflection

1. How would you feel if you knew your pastor or priest were gay or lesbian?

2. List the qualifications you feel are important for ordination. What characteristics make a person unfit for ordination?

3. Assuming gays and lesbians are not accepted as clergyper-

sons in your denomination, what do you think would happen if they were?

4. Do you think the "don't ask, don't tell, don't pursue" policy would be a good one for the church?

SUGGESTED RESOURCES

Glaser, Chris. *Uncommon Calling.* San Francisco: Harper & Row, 1988. And *Come Home! Reclaiming Spirituality and Community as Gay Men and Lesbians.* San Francisco: Harper & Row, 1990. Witness of a gay man called into Christian ministry.

Gramick, Jeannine, ed. *Homosexuality in the Priesthood and the Religious Life.* New York: Crossroad Publishing Co., 1989. Primarily personal stories and reflections of homosexually oriented priests and others committed to religious service.

Linscheid, John. "Beyond Ordination," *The Other Side,* July/August 1990, pp. 35-38. An openly gay Christian argues against the push for ordination of lesbians and gays, as acceptance of a heterosexist view that separates power between clergy and laity.

Lovelace, Richard. *Homosexuality and the Church.* Old Tappan, N.J.: Fleming H. Revell Co., 1978. Dated, but influential, conservative book speaking out against homosexuality and ordination.

Melton, J. Gordon, ed. *The Churches Speak on Homosexuality: Official Statements from Religious Bodies and Ecumenical Organizations.* Detroit: Gale Research, 1991.

CHAPTER 6

ARE GAY UNIONS CHRISTIAN COVENANTS?

Catherine Clark Kroeger

Chapter 6

E thical issues have often rocked churches. Less than 150 years ago, the Cape Cod town where I live was supported by seafaring trade, and there was bitter controversy over whether slave traders should be admitted to church membership. Most Christians nowadays would say that they should have accepted the *persons* but not the *practice*. When we come to the question of the legitimacy of same-sex unions as covenants, some have argued that the church should place its blessing on them just as it does on the marriage of a man and a woman. Such unions would be understood to be far removed from the promiscuity that characterizes some homosexual life-styles and would presumably constitute a faithful, monogamous, and permanent liaison.

Some churches already welcome such covenantal relationships, while others reflect on the issue more cautiously. Certainly, the Bible extols the friendship of Jonathan and David and the commitment of Ruth and Naomi. John describes himself as "the disciple whom Jesus loved." Paul knew deep bonding with both Barnabas and Silas, and Timothy was "his own true son." There is no evidence, however, that any of these relationships contained sexual elements. David found his affection for Jonathan more satisfying than the troubled relationships that he experienced with his wives. Naomi sent Ruth to sleep at Boaz's feet on the threshing floor, and Jesus spoke of those who made themselves eunuchs for the sake of the kingdom of heaven. The tender relationships were significant and enriching to many others among the people of God.

Today as then we can affirm strong bonding between persons of the same sex, commitment to each other, and a mutual resolve to serve God to the best of their ability. We can give strong and loving support to those within the family of God who share with us their orientation and intend to live as celibates. But should the church, the visible Body of Jesus Christ in this world, countenance an overtly *sexual* union as being ordained and blessed of God?

A Consideration of Covenants

Those of us who hold the Scriptures to be our guide in matters of faith and conduct must first reflect on the nature of biblical covenants: "All the ways of the LORD are loving and faithful/for those who keep the demands of/his covenant" (Ps. 25:10 NIV). Let us begin with the covenant made to Noah. To him and his wife, as well as to his sons and their wives (Gen. 9:9-16), it promised the preservation of humanity on the earth and the regular functioning of the earth's cycle. Sadly, humankind has often despised and abused this benefaction of God. Yet every time we see a rainbow, the visible sign of that covenant, we remember again the continuing mercies of God who will not break a promise.

Next followed the covenant with Abraham and Sarah as husband and wife, given new names and new identities as persons called and committed to God and to each other (Gen. 17:17-21). This covenant placed certain obligations on both human and divine members of the agreement (Gen. 15:9-21; 17:1-22). God promised progeny and land and a loving watchcare, while Abraham in turn was expected to see to it that all male offspring were circumcised. The sign of this covenant was not in the skies but in human flesh. God declared, "My covenant in your flesh is to be an everlasting covenant" (17:13 NIV). We may find it strange that the evidence of commitment was an earthly one, indeed a sexual one, but issues of sexuality and reproduction are highly prominent in virtually all of the Hebrew Bible.

It is no coincidence that the mark of the covenant was placed on the sexual organ of each male. The instrument that might be so tragically misused was instead dedicated to the holy purposes of God. This organ, which is external and visible, might more easily bear a sign of the covenant than could the feminine organ, which lies within a woman's body, concealed but receptive. Yet both men and women were called to comprise the covenant community, obedient to the claims of God on individual human lives.

Those same claims were paramount in the sign of the covenant given at Sinai, the observation of the Sabbath (Exod. 31:14-17; Ezek. 20:12-20). It entailed a systematic setting aside of one's legitimate priorities in response to a higher calling (Isa. 58:13-14). God promised a special inclusion within the covenant to persons deprived of sexual expression and yet faithful to the divine mandate of the Sabbath (Isa. 56:4-5).

Prominent within the covenant given to Moses was the establishment of very high standards of sexual conduct. Phinehas was given a "covenant of perpetual priesthood" specifically because of his concern for sexual purity within the congregation of Israel (Num. 25:2-13). The promise of the New Covenant given to Jeremiah was couched in terms of Yahweh the wife, as husband to Israel the reiteration of the conjugal relationship established at Sinai (Jer. 31:31-34).

The covenants promised health, offspring, and blessing as the fruit of sexual expressions conforming to the laws of God. Sexuality, revealed in Scripture as an enormously powerful force, can also do great harm. Particularly in Leviticus, we find a review of destructive expressions of sexuality, those types of behavior considered defiling not only to the individual but also to the community at large. Within the extended passage, homosexual activity is mentioned twice: "Do not lie with a man as one lies with a woman; that is detestable" (Lev. 18:22 NIV); and "If a man lies with a man as one lies with a woman, both of them have done what is detestable" (Lev. 20:13 NIV).

It is remarkable that this section of Leviticus regarding social and sexual behavior begins and ends with a reminder of God's covenant with Israel. Both sets of sexual instructions, those in chapter 18 and those in chapter 20, are accompanied with the declaration: "I am the LORD your God" (Lev. 18:2-5; 20:22-26)— precisely the terms in which the covenant was introduced at the giving of the Ten Commandments (Exod. 20:2). The text warns that the children of Israel must not behave as did the people of Egypt and Canaan or take their cues from the contemporary society, an instruction that was reiterated six times in chapter 18 (twice in v. 3, also in vv. 24, 26-27, 30). The section ends with these words: "You must not live according to the customs of the nations I am going to drive out before you. . . . I am the LORD your God, who has set you apart from the nations. . . . You are to be holy to me because I, the LORD, am holy, and I have set you apart from the nations to be my own" (Lev. 20:23-26 NIV).

When it comes to sexual behavior, we are asked to look at the holiness of God rather than current practice. Precisely because of the covenant, God's people were not to engage in certain sexual practices.

Same-Sex Marriages and New Testament Dictates

But many of the strictures of the Old Testament were no longer preserved in the New. Circumcision, for instance, was not required of male believers. Could not the New Covenant of love and grace include a place for homosexual marriage? It is sometimes argued that the New Testament did not address this question because same-sex marriages between mature, faithful adults were unknown. This is to ignore a substantial number of literary attestations for both male and female unions, for instance, those of the devoted pairs who composed the Theban army.

Centuries before the New Testament era, Plato had glorified permanent same-sex attachments. Such alliances, he said, made one a friend of God but were impeded by sexual expression (hence the expression "Platonic love"). Many such unions, however, were not celibate, and some were formalized with wedding ceremonies.[1] Even the binding words used in these rituals have been preserved in ancient texts. During the lifetime of the apostle Paul, same-sex marriages were in vogue at Rome, especially among young males of patrician families. Emperor Nero himself was said to have gone through two homosexual wedding ceremonies, once as the bride and once as the groom. The Egyptian princess Berenice "married Mesopotamia, and there was war between Garmos and Berenice on her account."[2] The New Testament writers could hardly have been ignorant of these societal patterns, especially in Paul's correspondence with the Roman church. Here he identifies both male and female homoerotic activity as lying outside the will and purposes of God (Rom. 1:26-27).

Sexuality as Communicative in the Covenant Community

All people are welcome in the household of God as they repent and seek newness of life. Certain behavioral patterns, however, are specifically rejected as being inappropriate for the family and kingdom of God. Throughout the Bible, there is a consistent theme that covenant people must maintain certain standards of behavior if they are to be included in the community (Gen. 17:14; Lev. 7:20-27; 20:2-3; Matt. 18:15-17; 1 Cor. 5:11; 2 Thess. 3:6).

Sex, although ostensibly a very private act, has repercussions on an extended circle of family, friends, coreligionists, and fellow citizens, a theme addressed in both Old and New Testaments. Preservation of sexual standards, it seems, has something to do with both covenant and community. What we do in private with our physical bodies can have a devastating effect on the spiritual community that is Christ's Body. We are members one of another, bound together, says Paul, and as such we have claims on one another.

In 1 Corinthians 6:13-20, he argues that joining the body of a believer with that of a prostitute means taking the members of the Body of Christ and making them members of a prostitute.

The text continues, "Flee sexual immorality. Every sin which an individual does is outside the body, but the one who is promiscuous sins within his/her body" (1 Cor. 6:18). As a small amount of leaven exerts its influence on the entire mass of dough (1 Cor. 5:6), so inappropriate sexual expression on the part of one member harms the corporate life of the whole.

Thus in 1 Corinthians 6:9-10, we find a repudiation of conduct that should not be tolerated within the household of faith: "Neither the sexually immoral nor idolaters nor adulterers, neither passive nor active partners in a homosexual relationship, nor thieves nor greedy nor drunkards nor verbally abusive nor rapists shall inherit the kingdom of God." We must, however, note that fornication, idolatry, adultery, thievery, greed, substance abuse, verbal abuse, rape, and extortion are similarly rejected in this same passage. Before this text, all of us stand condemned. Even as a believer, I confess with great sorrow that I have on occasion been untruthful, exploitive, verbally abusive, and greedy. I do not ask my sisters and brothers to affirm me in this behavior. Rather, I take my place beside my lesbian sisters and gay brothers in asking that the family of God support us as we seek to live a new and transformed life in Jesus Christ. I ask that they pray for us, encourage us, and guide us into higher paths of righteousness.

Our essential being is defined not by our actions or our sexual preferences but by our redemption in Christ. The biblical passage does not stop with excluding individuals whose behavior is unacceptable. After naming those who fall short of God's standards, Paul continues, "And such were some of you; but you were washed, but you were sanctified, but you were justified in the name of the Lord Jesus Christ, and in the Spirit of our God" (1 Cor. 6:11 NASB). God is in the business of making people new, and we are together heirs of the promise: "I will dwell among them and walk among them, and I will be their God, and they shall be my people. Therefore come out from among them and be separate, says the Lord, and do not touch the forbidden thing, and I will receive you, and I will be to you a father and you shall be to me sons and daughters" (2 Cor. 6:16-18).

Should Homosexual Persons Be Deprived of Sexual Expression and Meaningful Marriage?

But what of persons who feel no attraction to the opposite sex and would feel disbarred from a richly rewarding human relationship if the church does not affirm faithful same-sex marriage? Jesus renounced many legitimate needs in view of the higher priority of the claims of the Kingdom. The path to which Jesus called his followers was one of self-renunciation: "If anyone would come after me, let that one deny her or himself and take up her/his cross and follow me. Whoever wishes to save their life shall lose it, and whoever loses their life for my sake shall find it" (Matt. 16:24).

He denied himself food, sleep, and a permanent place of lodging, even though he called his followers to a concern precisely for hungry, poor, and homeless people. He challenged his disciples to a similar renunciation of their personal needs and desires in the all-consuming passion of commitment to the Good News of God's redemptive love. Not only did Jesus commend to his adherents fasting instead of food, watching instead of sleep, proclamation of the Kingdom rather than a fixed place of residence; but he pointed out that some had made themselves eunuchs for the sake of the kingdom of heaven (Matt. 19:12). In other words, they sacrificed active sexual expression for other values. He maintained that his claims and those of the gospel must be placed ahead of even legitimate family relationships, just as Isaiah had called on the people of Israel to set aside their priorities to do the will of God. This is not to say that Christ commended lifetime celibacy to all of his followers, but that sexual expression is not life's highest good or the only path for true fulfillment. A knowledge of God and a commitment to Jesus Christ take precedence over all else, even at the expense of personal risk and sacrifice.

Marriage as Covenant

Many issues involving the legitimacy of same-sex marriage (such as the adoption or custody of children) do not necessarily lie inside the household of faith and may more properly be debated within the forum of secular society. The biblical view is that both man and woman are necessary to reflect the image of God (Gen. 1:27; 5:1-2). Forming a household based on a sexually consummated marriage that is devoid of either male or female constitutes a deprivation. The apostle Paul declared, "Neither is the man without the woman nor the woman without the man, and all things are of God" (1 Cor. 11:11). He suggested that heterosexual marriage has within it a sanctifying power that extends to the children, even when one member is an unbeliever (1 Cor. 7:14).

Just as the covenant between God and Israel was often likened to the marriage of husband and wife, so also was Christ's relationship to the church. Human marriage, the union of man and woman—for all its frailty and fallibility—is designated by the Bible as a representation of the bond between God and ourselves as covenant people. Covenant involves community, not just the two individuals bound in a marriage. In the Hebrew Bible, we read that marriage was regarded as a covenant to which God was a witness (Prov. 2:17; Ezek. 16:8; Mal. 2:14). A man's wife was "[his] companion and [his] wife by covenant. Did not one God make her? Both flesh and spirit are his" (Mal. 2:14-15).

The Bible recognizes marriage as a covenant that includes one man and one woman and excludes others: "Therefore shall a man leave father and mother and cleave unto his wife." It involves both a leaving and a cleaving. So far as I know, this is the only sexual covenant within the believing community that warrants the distancing of two people from all the others. Its result will often be the establishment of a new generation of faith and new leadership within the family of God.

Both the Hebrew Bible and the New Testament celebrate the loyalty and devotion of same-sex commitment, but both stop short of an endorsement of genital expression. The Christian gay or lesbian is invited not to form an exclusive union with one other person of the same sex but, as someone committed to the will of God, to give oneself fully to the caring, loving, supporting, and affirming community of faith. In turn, the Bible directs believers to develop deep bonds of prayerful and supportive intimacy with homosexual persons who have chosen a life of celibacy. Regardless of sexual preference, all persons who receive Jesus Christ as Savior and Lord are part of the family of God; and together we must seek ways to integrate all believers into lives of obedience and conformity to God's will.

NOTES

1. Claudius Ptolemaeus *Tetrabiblios* 3.13.172; Lucian *Dialogues of Courtesans* 5.1-3; *Papyri Graecae Magicae* 32:1-19, 46.32.1-19; Ovid *Metamorphoses* 9.762-64.

2. Iamblichus *Babylonica*, summarized in Photius *Bibliotheca* 94.77a.20-24; 94.77b.32-38.

ARE GAY UNIONS CHRISTIAN COVENANTS?

Chris Glaser

Chapter 6

rge me not to leave you, or to return from following you; for where you go, I will go; and where you lodge, I will lodge; your people shall be my people, and your God my God; where you die, I will die, and there will I be buried. The Lord do so to me [an unrecorded chopping motion to the neck or additional curse would have been added at this point], and more also, if anything but death parts me from you. (Ruth to Naomi, Ruth 1:16-17 Amplified)

The soul of Jonathan was knit with the soul of David, and Jonathan loved him as his own life. . . . Then Jonathan made a covenant with David, because he loved him as his own life.

. . . David arose from beside the heap of stones, and fell on his face to the ground, and bowed himself three times. And they kissed one another, and wept with one another, until David got control of [literally, "exceeded"] himself. And Jonathan told David, Go in peace, forasmuch as we have sworn both of us in the name of the Lord, saying, The Lord shall be between me and you, between my descendants and yours forever. (1 Samuel 18:1, 3; 20:41-42 Amplified)

When serving on a national church task force on homosexuality in the late seventies, I witnessed a turning point toward greater acceptance when we heard the testimony of a gay couple who had celebrated their long-term relationship in a ceremony of their home church. Even persons on our committee who adamantly opposed the acceptance of homosexuality sat in quiet reverence after each testified of their shared life and faith and church commitment. One female committee member turned to me and whispered in awe, "They're so gentle."

Yet, to avoid controversy, our task force refrained from making any recommendations that the church explore the formulation of a liturgy solemnizing gay relationships. We had been asked to offer a recommendation on the ordination of "self-affirming, practicing homosexuals." In our regional hearings on the subject, the concept of gay or lesbian covenants seemed to reap more expressions of shock and disdain than ordination. Apparently, marriage was considered more sacrosanct.

During one hearing, a pastor proudly described to our task force that he had "successfully" broken up a lesbian relationship of many years' duration by threatening them with God's condemnation, while another pastor condemned gays and lesbians for their inability to establish long-term relationships! The church does not seem to understand that it presently endorses promiscuity by failing to support and celebrate same-gender unions. The alternative of celibacy cannot fairly be offered to gays and lesbians if they do not have the equivalent option of marriage.

Many people who oppose lesbian and gay covenants refer to one or both Creation stories in Genesis 1–2 as evidence that God created Adam and Eve, not Adam and Steve. (I like to point out that though the Garden of Eden story of agrarian bliss does not specifically mention factory workers or urban dwellers, they are no less valued by God!)

The purpose of the story of Adam and Eve is not to invalidate other covenants but to suggest two potential reasons for a covenant relationship: procreation and companionship. In Protestant theology, either reason validates a marriage, which is why contraceptive devices pose no threat to the benefactors of the Reformation, as contrasted with Roman Catholics, whose theology requires procreative possibility to justify every sexual encounter. Based on companionship or mutuality alone, lesbian or gay covenants could be justified.

An organization within my denomination would return Christians to "biblical sexuality." But I believe the members of that group would be horrified if we returned to the common practice of polygamy and the use of concubines in the Old Testament. King Solomon, an extreme example, had seven hundred wives and three hundred concubines (1 Kings 11:1-3). Old Testament writers viewed women and children as property, and marriage as an economic institution that, among other things, was necessary for matters of inheritance. Those views remained unquestioned until recent centuries.

The New Testament presents Jesus as less concerned for biological families than for the family of faith: "And he replied, 'Who are my mother and my brothers?' And looking at those who sat around him, he said, 'Here are my mother and my brothers! Whoever does the will of God is my brother and sister and mother' " (Mark 3:33-35). He called the disciples away from their families to fulfill the claims of God's inbreaking kingdom, a new world order. Jesus warned,

> Do not think that I have come to bring peace to the earth;
> I have not come to bring peace, but a sword.
> For I have come to set a man against his father,
> and a daughter against her mother,
> and a daughter-in-law against her mother-in-law;
> and one's foes will be members of one's own household.
> (Matt. 10:34-36)

That is hardly what we would think of when we hear "traditional family values" touted as biblical by some American Christians.

Women were among Jesus' disciples; children were allowed to come unto him. The early Christian community modeled a changing attitude toward women in leadership roles, and welcomed the membership of Gentiles who didn't subscribe to the Law of Moses.

At the same time, the apostle Paul maligned marriage, while

endorsing men's ownership ("lordship") of women in marriage. Jesus' teaching against heterosexual divorce has been conveniently reinterpreted or set aside, though ironically, it is often quoted in opposition to same-gender marriage: "Have you not read that the one who made them at the beginning 'made them male and female,' and said, 'For this reason a man shall leave his father and mother and be joined to his wife, and the two shall become one flesh'?" (Matt. 19:4-5).

Yet the meaning of what Jesus says about eunuchs within the same text is ignored: neither procreative possibility nor opposite-gender marriage is required for admission to the kingdom of heaven. Jesus told his disciples, "Not everyone can accept this teaching, but only those to whom it is given. For there are eunuchs who have been so from birth, and there are eunuchs who have been made eunuchs by others, and there are eunuchs who have made themselves eunuchs for the sake of the kingdom of heaven" (Matt. 19:11-12).

No scholarly analysis is required for a reader of Scripture to see that same-gender covenants are lifted up as models for relationships in the Bible. Ruth's willingness to leave her country, culture, and theology to adopt her mother-in-law Naomi's country, culture, and theology as her own exemplifies the very heart of love, so much so that her vow cited at the beginning of this section is often used at opposite-gender weddings.

Jonathan, whose own father, King Saul, angrily accused him of choosing David "to your own shame, and to the shame of your mother's nakedness" (1 Sam. 20:30), willingly gave up his right to fight for the throne out of love for David, an unnatural sacrifice of male power. Since control issues are central to any relationship of equals, this willingness to compromise and sacrifice may guide both same-gender and opposite-gender couples. "Your love to me was wonderful, passing the love of women" (2 Sam. 1:26), David mournfully eulogized his fallen comrade.

If the covenants between Ruth and Naomi and David and Jonathan were validated and blessed and heralded in Scripture, what prevents the church from validating and blessing and heralding same-gender covenants today? Lesbian and gay covenants imply sexuality, and a sexuality that is different from the majority—both taboo topics. The church's theology of sexuality inadequately celebrates sexual pleasure as a means of God's grace and inadequately accommodates inherent sexual difference as a manifestation of God's diverse creation.

A scholar has discovered that it has not always been so, having found numerous examples of same-gender bonding buried in church history. History professor John Boswell of Yale University awed the academic world with the publication of his book *Christianity, Social Tolerance, and Homosexuality,* which revealed that the church has not always been intolerant of homosexuality. Later, a priest requesting anonymity drew Boswell's attention to a rite of spiritual friendship performed by the church for same-gender couples. Reflecting years of thorough academic research in the United States and Europe, Boswell's tentatively titled *Same-Sex Unions in Pre-Modern Europe* will reveal that same-gender union liturgies predated and coexisted with opposite-gender church marriages. For nearly the first half of the church's existence, marriages were civil rather than religious affairs. Since they were usually private, a dissolution could easily be obtained by persuading the few witnesses to disclaim the marriage had occurred. To stop this practice, marriages were moved into churches, where there would be too many witnesses to bribe.

Two friends of mine, one of whom is a medieval historian like Boswell, invited me to preside at their own "Rite of Spiritual Brotherhood" based on the ancient ceremony. A centerpiece of the liturgy, which was performed by the church for women as well as men, is the invocation of the names, love, and martyrdom of two saints, Sergius and Bacchus, who share the same feast day of October 7.

Segius and Bacchus were soldiers in the Roman army in the late third and early fourth centuries. Favorites of Emperor Maximian, they fell into disfavor when they refused to worship the emperor's idols and confessed their Christian faith. According to Boswell, the texts describing their relationship use a word that translates "lovers." This seems confirmed by their initial punishment, ridiculed while paraded through city streets in women's clothing.

As a sign of unity, they sang together Psalm 23, changing the "I" wording to "we" language, which became a part of the later rite. Tortured, Bacchus died, but appeared to Segius in a vision in prison. Radiant, Bacchus told Sergius that they were "bound together" forever and would be reunited, and that "your crown of justice is me, my crown of justice is you." After additional torture, Sergius was beheaded. One chronicler described them: "They were as one in the love of Jesus Christ and inseparable as spiritual brothers. They were like stars shining joyously over the earth, radiating the light of profession of and faith in our savior and Lord Jesus Christ."[1]

The prayers from the rite describe God as having "willed that your holy martyrs Sergius and Bacchus be joined by a bond not of nature, but of faith and the Holy Spirit" and entreat on behalf of the couple to be united, "since your servants have already been joined to one another in spiritual love, we ask you to grant them a faith unconfounded, and a love without pretense."[2]

The church family itself, joined as it were by a bond "not of nature, but of faith and the Holy Spirit," would do well to consider the faith and Spirit within couples seeking same-gender unions. Then with "a faith unconfounded" by heterosexism (the narrow heterosexual view of the world), the church might *offer* "a love without pretense," that is, a love that does not require either hypocrisy or heterosexuality, as well as *celebrate* "a love without pretense," that is, uncloseted lesbian and gay covenant unions.

NOTES

1. *Catholic Encyclopedia* and the lectures of Dr. John Boswell for the Lazarus Project of the West Hollywood Presbyterian Church, Los Angeles, California.

2. Prayers from the Greek *Euchologion*, ed. Jacobus Goar, trans. Mark Infusino (Paris, 1647).

STUDY GUIDE

Increasing numbers of gay and lesbian persons are asking the church to provide a formal, public service by which their commitment to each other can be affirmed and blessed in the eyes of God and the community of faith. Denominational practices vary, but a majority prohibit clergypersons from performing same-sex marriages or unions.

Catherine Clark Kroeger buttresses the church's stance against endorsing same-sex unions by citing Scripture, particularly affirming that marriage was intended only to bring together males and females. Chris Glaser emphasizes same-sex friendships in the Bible and points to forgotten church traditions, when in the past same-sex relationships were blessed by the church.

Items for Reflection

1. What does it mean to enter into the covenant of marriage?

2. How should gay and lesbian couples express their love, concern, and faithfulness for each other?

3. Do you think the acceptance of gay unions by the church would help homosexual persons lead more secure and stable lives?

4. How realistic do you think a lifetime of celibacy would be for you or for people you know, heterosexual and homosexual?

5. How do you feel about gay and lesbian persons entering heterosexual marriages and trying to fit into the cultural mainstream?

SUGGESTED RESOURCES

Berzon, Betty. *Permanent Partners: Building Gay and Lesbian Relationships That Last.* New York: E. P. Dutton, 1988. Written by a therapist, this book suggests dynamics operative in long-term relationships.

Boswell, John. *Christianity, Social Tolerance, and Homosexuality.* Chicago: University of Chicago Press, 1980. Winner of 1981 American Book Award for History, it probes the rise of homophobia in church and society in the late Middle Ages. Also see John Boswell, *Same-Sex Unions in Pre-Modern Europe* (forthcoming).

Hays, Richard B. "Relations Natural and Unnatural: A Response to John Boswell's Exegesis of Romans 1." *The Journal of Religious Ethics* 4 (Spring 1986). Argues Paul condemns homosexuality and contends John Boswell's interpretation of Romans 1 is flawed at key points.

Stott, John. "Homosexual Partnerships: Why Same Sex Relationships Are Not a Christian Option." In *Involvement*, pp. 215-44. Old Tappan, N.J.: Fleming H. Revell Co., 1985.

Stuart, Elizabeth. *Daring to Speak Love's Name.* London: Hamish Hamilton, 1992. Discusses liturgies that celebrate gay and lesbian relations.

HOW SHOULD THE CHURCH MINISTER TO HOMOSEXUAL PERSONS AND THEIR FAMILIES?

Riley B. Case

Chapter 7

Margaret shocked her church community when she divorced her pastor husband and moved with one of the women in the congregation to a city several states away. Although there was no public explanation, Margaret shared with a few acquaintances that she could be happy only in a relationship with another woman.

Joan was a faithful member of the youth group and well liked by everyone. She developed a close relationship with another girl, which soon became characterized by extreme jealousy and possessiveness. She was able to talk freely with the pastor, and together they sought to explore the possibility of homosexuality. The situation was extremely upsetting to her.

Tom became involved in homosexual behavior in high school. His years in an evangelical college were accompanied by periods of guilt and depression. Through counseling and the support of Christian friends, he was able to overcome his feelings of guilt and depression. He married a Christian woman and became a medical missionary.

Beth and Steve are teenagers without father or mother. After their father died, they learned his death was AIDS-related. Their father had contracted AIDS through his secret homosexual life.

Their mother contracted AIDS from their father and also died from an AIDS-related disease. Because there was such family shame, only a few persons in the church knew the whole story.

These particular incidents involving homosexuality are not atypical in the life of the church. For years Christians have either denied the existence of homosexuality within the church or responded to homosexuality as an anathema too horrible to behold. The church's response has been to its own discredit.

In one way or another the church must be involved. The question is how?

This discussion examines two assumptions underlying the church's perspective on ministry to homosexual persons and their families. The first assumption is that the biblical and traditional understandings of human sexuality are not only valid for our time but are also crucial for maintaining the integrity of the Christian message. Marriage between a man and a woman is an integral part of the order of creation, linked with the fulfillment of personhood and the replenishing of the earth.

Marriage between a man and a woman is also an integral part of the orders of redemption, serving as a witness to the faithfulness that underlies God's covenant with his people and the mystical union between Christ and the church, and anticipating the New Creation associated with the end of all things (Rev. 21:1-2). For this and other reasons the fullness of sexual intimacy is to be reserved within the marriage of a man and a woman. Outside the marriage bond we are called to celibacy.

The second assumption is that the church is a called-out people with a mission and ministry different from those of all other communities, institutions, and agencies. There may be areas of overlap and cooperation with these other communities and agencies, but essentially, the church is in a different business. Because Christians have different values and a different set of ethics, the church will differ from the world in the understanding of the purpose and nature of human existence. The church may draw insights from disciplines such as psychology or sociology, but these insights are interpreted in the light of Christian faith.

The theological basis of ministry for evangelical pastors and churches begins with the central truth of the gospel: that God has graciously acted on our behalf in Jesus Christ. The setting for God's action is this present fallen world. The doctrine of original sin is the church's effort to explain the brokenness of humanity in which persons and societies are alienated from God, others, self, and the creation, and in need of redemption or salvation.

The good news is that this salvation is now available in Jesus Christ. Christ died for our sins, was buried, and rose from the dead (1 Cor. 15:3-4) in order to reconcile us with the Father. Through repentance and faith, we are born again, becoming new creatures in Christ, joined as a people in a New Covenant to God's healing presence in the world, to the end that all things might ultimately be united in Christ, in heaven and on earth.

The Christian believer is a member of two worlds: the present fallen world and world system and a new world order, the kingdom of God. The ministry to homosexual persons and their families can best be understood in the context of the interaction between these two world systems and an understanding of the working of God's grace.

This working of God's grace may be discussed on three levels: prevenient grace, justifying grace, and sanctifying grace.

Prevenient Grace

Prevenient grace, or common grace, or preparing grace, is the gift that enables us to respond to God's love for us. Even in our fallen state, and despite the pervasiveness of sin, there is given to each of us an innate sense of right and wrong, a desire for a more fulfilling life, and a freedom to make moral choices.

One should not kill, steal, commit adultery, or bear false witness. There is a decency that ought to be in order for all peoples and all societies. On this level, we can argue for a certain level of morality in civil law.

But on another level, we recognize a Christian ethic, an ethic of the Kingdom, that goes beyond justice and decency, and speaks in categories of love, mercy, forgiveness, and holy living. The church's argument for sexual purity differs from that of society in general.

Scriptures remind Christians that our bodies are temples of the Holy Spirit, that fornication is a form of idolatry, and that references to "holy and without blemish" and "without a spot or wrinkle" (Eph. 5:27) refer not only to the relationship between Christ and his church but also to the relationship between a man and a woman in marriage. The church seeks to model this new kingdom ethic, individually among its members, and in its common life together.

It is not at all certain, or desirable, that the church should seek to impose this ethic as civil law or even as the prevailing cultural mores. It is workable, simply because the world operates from entirely different presuppositions about the nature of human existence and the meaning of life.

The argument for sexual purity for the general society is based on the God-given sense of decency and respect for all persons associated with prevenient grace and goes something like this: there is in the nature of things an implied emotional and spiritual bonding in sexual intimacy. Sexual promiscuity easily exploits the other's vulnerability, undermines the institution of the family, and contributes to the breakdown of the basic trust on which the moral fabric of society rests. And quite coincidentally, it is associated with the spread of sexually transmitted diseases.

Sexual intimacy should be reserved for marriage between a man and a woman. This traditional sexual morality is currently being challenged from many quarters. The prevailing sexual ethic in society, with its emphasis on responsible sex or safe sex or consenting adults or "if it's fun, do it" or "it's right if nobody gets hurt," undermines the traditional emphasis on faithfulness in marriage and celibacy in singleness. In this debate the church is often characterized as puritanical, morally rigid, and irrelevant.

In this situation the church must resist the temptation to

become defensive and self-righteous. In a fallen world, even Christians will disagree in matters of minimum human morality. The church must make its witness even while respecting and loving persons with whom it disagrees. This includes upholding the dignity of practicing gays and lesbians. Whatever the church has to offer through counseling, classes, worship, or food pantries must be shared without regard to political affiliation, social standing, ethnic or racial background, or sexual orientation.

While the church ministers without regard to response, at the same time it never shies away from making known the person of Jesus Christ. The evangelistic motive behind the church's ministries may not always be apparent, but it is always there, with the realization that any reaching out to meet human need is inadequate if it does not address the greatest need of all, the spiritual need to be reconciled to a loving God.

Justifying Grace

A second form of grace, justifying grace, is the gift of God that, on the basis of faith, forgives and receives us despite our failures, sins, and shortcomings. Because of the blood of Jesus Christ, we are saved from the consequences of sin: the wrath of God, hell, and eternal death.

The biblical doctrine of justification by grace through faith is a truth that distinguishes Christianity from other religious systems. If justification is not by works, by meeting some standard, even the biblical moral standard, if it is not granted because of some righteousness within us or anything we have earned, there can be no sense of boasting or self-righteousness within us.

It is at this point that the church has consistently and tragically failed through the years. The feeling is sometimes expressed, and often felt even when not expressed, that the church is judgmental and does not want me if I am "not good enough."

The conflict between Paul and the Judaizers is still with us. Must one achieve some minimum standard of righteousness to be acceptable to God and, by extension, the church? The church's answer is (or at least should be) that the righteousness that makes us acceptable is the righteousness of Christ. We are loved unconditionally even when we stumble time after time. The Gospels are full of the accounts of previously unacceptable persons—prostitutes and tax collectors—who discovered this truth in Jesus.

Because of the church's failure at this point, it is understandable that numbers of people, including homosexual persons, feel alienated from the very people who claim to embody the truth of God's love. While many of us are not comfortable with the term *homophobia* because it has become a political bludgeon, there is present, even in the church, an unhealthy fear or hatred of homosexual persons.

But there is an opposite danger, also. In proclaiming that salvation is by grace, and not by works, or by meeting some standard, we are tempted to suggest that God's high moral standards, including the call for sexual purity, are really not that important. In an effort to be accepting, we have sometimes become tolerant to the point of moral indifference.

Anything short of God's high standard for holy living, including sexual purity, is sin. We all approach God's presence in need of justifying grace. We all fall short of God's glory. As God's love is extended to all, so is the church's. In terms of practical ministry to homosexual persons and their families, the church must be open to all. We must struggle continually against judgmentalism. But at the same time we do not bless or condone the sin. We do not condone the practice of homosexuality, but at the same time we do not condone the sin of racism or homophobia or a self-righteous attitude.

At this point there is a need for still another kind of grace.

Sanctifying Grace

A third kind of grace is sanctifying grace. The word *salvation* carries the idea of escape (from the consequences of sin), but it also carries the idea of wholeness. There is a future and otherworldly dimension of salvation, but there is also a present and this-worldly dimension. The New Testament is full of references to the call upon us to be "conformed to the image of his Son," "changed unto his likeness," to live lives free from the principalities and powers of this present age. The work of God associated with the purity of heart and life is called "sanctifying grace."

God's sanctifying grace works through personal discipline and obedience, but it also works through the life of the church, through the sacraments, through worship and study and caring fellowship. When the church is at its best, it offers the vision of a better life, and the accountability and support that enables God's sanctifying grace to bring that life into existence.

It is then that the church becomes truly a hospital for the cure of souls. Whatever the addiction, whatever the compulsion, whatever the bondage, there can be healing in Jesus. The result is a work of God leading to new levels of spiritual awareness and a desire to live a life-style (the ethic of the Kingdom) yielded to Christ and empowered by the Holy Spirit.

How this translates into practical ministry in regard to human sexuality varies from situation to situation. Such a practical ministry calls for time with children and teenagers exploring issues of sexuality from the perspective of the Christian understanding of human nature and holy living. It means time in learning and caring groups dealing with home and family issues, in husband-wife and parent-children relationships. It means being available for persons with unresolved pain in their lives because of abuse or broken marriages or addictions. It also means holding persons responsible for their failures and for their need to live the holy life God has intended.

For homosexual persons and their families, it means holding out always the truth that justification is by grace through faith, not on the basis of any standard of righteousness. It means supporting and caring and loving, no matter what a person's sexual orientation or moral failures. But it also means holding up always the Christian ideal of a holy life, and the encouragement and support to live that life. In some cases, that might mean the encouragement and support to live a celibate life. In other cases, that might mean offering the confidence that marriage vows between a man and a woman can be faithfully upheld.

No one will claim that ministry with homosexual persons is easy, or that it has often been carried out successfully. Some homosexual persons and their families will reject this vision of ministry. Others, however, will respond to its message of grace and hope.

Margaret continues in a committed lesbian relationship with her friend and is active in church and community.

Joan did finally face a number of problems in her life, including an unusual home situation, sexual abuse, and her homosexuality. She is now living in a lesbian relationship.

Tom struggled with homosexuality throughout his life, but his marriage and family held together.

Beth and Steve are coping with the help of Christian friends.

The church was present in each instance, sometimes in commendable ways, sometimes not. But God's grace extends to the church, also, as it seeks to be faithful to its task.

HOW SHOULD THE CHURCH MINISTER TO HOMOSEXUAL PERSONS AND THEIR FAMILIES?

Larry Kent Graham

A Personal Journey Toward Care

Chapter 7

I grew up in southern California in the forties and fifties. It was a macho era. I did not know persons who identified themselves as gay or lesbian. I was taught to fear them as "perverts" who might take abusive advantage of me. When after high school I went to a Lutheran Bible school in New Jersey, I met Bill, a gay man from Queens, New York. He was avowedly gay, and he spent many weekends in New York City living an actively gay life. We became friends, and the somewhat conservative Christian environment provided a warm and safe place for him. He did not feel a contradiction between his orientation and his Christian faith, though he was rightly worried about the consequences of his life-style for his health and for his future in the church.

I found myself personally confronted by Bill and the Bible school environment. We were being taught in the Lutheran context that God's grace was sufficient; that no person is saved or damned by works or the quality of his or her life, but by God's sheer mercy and faithfulness. I deeply believed this, and I struggled with its challenge to my fear, ignorance, and stereotyping of Bill's sexual orientation and life-style. A close friendship evolved. I learned a great deal about myself, and I became freer to appreciate and learn from persons who were quite different from me. I became less frightened of my sexuality and that of others. I became opposed to those who denigrated Bill and people like him; I felt committed to the welfare of my friend as an expression of the gospel of God's love.

I agonized with my friend's struggle to affirm himself in the face of the estrangement arising from persons who said he was evil and condemned for something he could do nothing about. I was grateful for the Bible school environment whose faculty and staff provided a caring and welcoming environment for him, however mixed the affirmation sometimes appeared to be. I identified with his efforts to find relationships that enhanced rather than demeaned him. For me, my friendship with Bill in the gospel-centered Christian community was a foundational experience of pastoral caregiving and care-receiving with a gay brother. It still shapes what I believe to be essential for pastoral care with all persons, especially gays and lesbians. It informs much of the following discussion.

Care as Restoration and Opposition

The overall purpose of pastoral care in the Christian church is to increase the love of God, self, and neighbor, to promote justice, and to enhance vital partnerships between humans and nature.[1] Since the essence of God's being is loving communion in freedom, when just and loving relationships emerge in a fertile, dynamic, and harmonious world, the being and will of God are actualized.[2] Therefore, the fundamental concern of pastoral care is to restore persons to the image of God as reflected in an increased capacity for communion with all of life and to a joyful relationship with God. This is the restorative or healing dimension of care.

There is also an oppositional dimension of care. Christian pastoral care has a prophetic responsibility that calls into account every factor in the world that works against self-regard and love of God and neighbor. It seeks to set aside unjust structures of oppression and exploitation, and it discerns and undermines patterns of ecological rapaciousness. Christian pastoral care works against these forces wherever they appear, even when the church itself perpetuates them.

It is the thesis of this essay that when gay men and lesbian women seek pastoral care in the church, like all other persons seeking care, they desire to overcome all that works against their capacity to love themselves uniquely as God loves them and to find a joyful relationship with their creator and redeemer. They, too, seek to overcome barriers to the call to love their neighbors and to promote just partnerships and harmonious relationships between humans and the natural order. Pastoral care to lesbian women and gay men therefore requires that the caregiving community and its representatives, both lay and ordained, embody love, justice, and ecologically viable practices in their responses. Concretely, the caregiving community and its representatives must provide a context of solidarity with gay and lesbian persons that combines supportive, healing, and restorative measures with prophetic challenge to itself and to the world that perpetrates lovelessness and injustice toward them.

Healing and Solidarity in Community

If God has created us as fellow humans to be in loving community with one another, to be enemies and strangers is against the will of God. Bill and the Bible school provided a basis for me to understand that love casts out fear of one another and that all parties are enriched by sustained and intense disclosure of the inner being in an environment where the gospel's affirmation is dominant. To care for gay and lesbian persons—to love them justly—means to know and to be in solidarity with the *particularity* of their humanity. In the pastoral care context, this, first of all, means to listen to their pain and to support aspirations for their unique fulfillment in loving fellowship. In the public arena, it means to oppose anything that reduces their unique and particular humanity to a stereotype or to dissolve it into a denigrated or marginalized class of persons.

An example of listening to pain and supporting aspirations for a person's unique fulfillment in a relationship of solidarity became poignantly clear to me a few years ago when a minister of twenty years sought me out to discuss his long-standing depression.* "William Carroll" reported that he had had psychiatric treatment for years to handle this depression, but with only partial success. He went on to disclose that he thought that he was probably gay and that his depression was related to his failed attempts to deny his gayness and to live in the closet as a married father of two children and as a minister in a mainline congregation. He was in a great deal of pain as he shared his struggles to deny, contain, and overcome his homosexuality through therapy, abstinence, work, and marriage. He was mortified that he had on occasion read gay literature and sought out sexual liaisons with other men. He sobbed when he realized that for years he had preached about a God who accepted us as we are, but that he himself had never felt that acceptance.

I listened for some time as he poured out his story. I said little. He came to the point in the conversation where he said, "You are the first person other than a therapist with whom I have shared all of this. Thank you for listening. I think I have to decide whether to make some changes in my life. I can't keep living like this." He went on to say that it was scary to think of telling his wife because he knew that the marriage would have to end: "She deserves more than this; though I love her, it is difficult to feel positively about our sexual relationship. She is unhappy with it, too, and there is no likelihood that it will ever improve." He also knew that he would probably have to leave his congregation and community, since they were situated in such a manner that it would be difficult to maintain his ministry in the face of a divorce, much less a revelation of his gay orientation. He worried that he might have to leave the ministry alto-

---

* The pastoral stories in this chapter are modified to assure anonymity; they are shared with permission.

gether. On that point he was ambivalent. On the one hand, he thought that it would be a relief not to have to live a lie any longer; he had an avocational interest in counseling by which he could earn a living. On the other hand, he had been a highly effective minister, and he did not want to relinquish his calling to serve others and to preach the gospel. I suggested that it was probably too early to make any decisions, but that it might be better to live with his self-disclosure about his gayness and see what unfolded naturally.

After our meeting, his life began to move rapidly. He later said that he cried the entire three hours driving home. He felt a mixture of relief, pain, and terror. For the first time, when he looked at himself in the mirror, he saw a person who could affirm that he was a gay man. Simultaneously, he realized for the very first time when he gazed in the mirror that he saw a man whom God loved. He was profoundly moved by the experience. Within a year, his depression lifted, he and his wife amicably divorced, he confided his homosexuality to his children who affirmed him, and he extended his ministry to working with persons living with AIDS, and their families, in his community. Within three years, he had relocated to another ministry setting in which persons hiring him were aware of his gayness, though he has not come out of the closet. I saw him intermittently through that period, mostly offering pastoral support and encouragement and listening to the events of his life as they unfolded. We have continued to remain in touch after his move to another part of the country where we have mutual friends. His wife has subsequently remarried. He is rebuilding his life and conducting his ministry in an authentic and fulfilling manner.

I believe that in Reverend Carroll's story we see in concrete and particular terms the process of overcoming estrangement and being restored to the image of God as a direct consequence of supportive pastoral care by a representative of a community that is in solidarity with the unique aspirations of gay people. He was able to live the truth rather than a lie, and to find that God is a God of reconciliation from estrangement when the truth is faced in a caring environment. Rather than live in isolation and falsehood with his family and others, he was freed to live the truth in love and to promote increased patterns of loving in his family and in his religious communities. His love for God became more intense, and his sense of God's love became real rather than empty. Through the ministry of care, mediated by honesty in mutual self-disclosure, he is being restored to the image of God as a gay man. From this base and its subsequent benefits, he was further able to reach out in communion with others. He has also been able to publicly oppose dominant antigay theological perspectives in the church. His article in *The Christian Century*, "God as Unloving Father," is a gripping retelling of the story of the prodigal son from a gay perspective.[3] It is a strong example of how his personal liberation to love in the ministry of care has contributed to a prophetic witness.

A second requirement of pastoral care in solidarity with the *particular* humanity of gay and lesbian persons involves listening for the presence of God in their lives, especially in relation to despair and self-hatred generated by the rejecting church and culture. It is often psychologically and spiritually intolerable for gay persons—especially gay adolescents—to sustain the secret knowledge of their identity in a punitive and cruel environment. Care requires that we hear this pain and discern the sustaining presence of God by providing acceptance and nurture. The importance of this is well illustrated in the story of Anne, a lesbian woman who writes of her adolescence:

> From age 13-17 I found myself tortured by the pain I carried within. Because of my identity, I found myself isolated and alone. Tears seemed my closest companion during those years. I cried many an hour, alone in my room. I longed for someone to tell me that I was okay and loved. As I think back on those times, I wonder how I *ever* made it through. How did I avoid hopelessness and despair? Truth is, I didn't. At one point, I drove a car off the road in an attempt to take my life. At the last minute, I skidded to a stop between two pines. I waited many years to tell anyone about that day. I was embarrassed that I had considered suicide—embarrassed that I would ever feel so hopeless.

When asked how she survived that period, this daughter of a minister in a small rural town said, "Rebellion. I survived by wearing an exterior that did not need 'their support' and 'their validation.' I survived alone, with God's grace and compassion to see me through." At her most acute period, when a friend had taken her in after her parents' rejection forced her to leave home, God spoke to her with these words: "I love you my child; don't let them come between us." At that moment, she "found the hope to resist despair; I found 'home' in God's companionship." Her Creator had become her companion and redeemer; she was restored to self-love and to a joyful and firm love of God, which has sustained her since that time. Her friend's hospitality and affirmation, I believe, were essential for this resistance and restoration.

Conclusion

Pastoral care of gay and lesbian persons calls the caregiver and the caregiving community to let the gospel of affirmation and solidarity heal isolation and oppose rejection. The gospel changes what we view as normative and sacred, and changes the way we view our fellow humans. Like Jesus in the grain fields on the Sabbath, it calls us to make concrete human welfare and specific physical needs and energies, rather than sacral traditions and interpretations, the motivational center of our lives (Matt. 12:1-14). To some this is an outrage—even as it was in Jesus' day. To Jesus, and to God, it is the central requirement of the gospel, and the essential requirement for restorative and oppositional caregiving with, and on behalf of, lesbian and gay persons.

NOTES

1. For a fuller discussion of this definition, see Larry Kent Graham, *Care of Persons, Care of Worlds: A Psychosystems Approach to Pastoral Care and Counseling* (Nashville: Abingdon Press, 1992).

2. This view of the image of God is reflected in much contemporary

theology. See, for example, Daniel Day Williams, *The Spirit and the Forms of Love* (New York: Harper & Row, 1968), and Rosemary Radford Ruether, *Sexism and God Talk: Toward a Feminist Theology* (Boston: Beacon Press, 1983).

3. "William Carroll," "God as Unloving Father," *The Christian Century,* March 6, 1991, p. 255.

STUDY GUIDE

Authors in this book do not favor excluding gay and lesbian persons from participation and membership in the life of the church. While they disagree about ordination and same-sex unions, they generally encourage an active ministry to homosexual persons and their families.

Riley Case upholds the traditional "love the sinner, hate the sin" stance, which rejects homosexual behavior but affirms homosexual persons. Larry Kent Graham contends pastoral care's concern restores persons "to the image of God" by affirming the person's sexual orientation and by prophetically challenging oppressive theologies and structures that deny full human dignity to gays and lesbians.

Items for Reflection

1. Christians often assert that they "love the sinner but hate the sin." Can one really distinguish so clearly?

2. Should gay and lesbian persons have equal rights in terms of employment, housing, insurance, and so on? Do laws that protect homosexual persons from discrimination involve basic "civil" rights or "special" rights?

3. Homosexuality used to be widely considered a crime even among consenting adults. Some states still have laws to that effect on their books, but they are seldom enforced. What should the church's stance be in regard to so-called sodomy laws?

4. How do you and your church respond to openly homosexual persons or parents of gays and lesbians who choose to participate in your congregation?

5. A large percentage of adolescents who contemplate suicide

struggle with concerns related to homosexuality. What would you say to a teenager who has concluded that it is better to be dead than gay or lesbian?

SUGGESTED RESOURCES

Graham, Larry Kent. *Care of Persons, Care of Worlds: A Psychosystems Approach to Pastoral Care and Counseling.* Nashville: Abingdon Press, 1992.

Hilton, Bruce. *Can Homophobia Be Cured? Wrestling with Questions That Challenge the Church.* Nashville: Abingdon Press, 1991. Explores question of what the church does with the increasing realization that gays and lesbians are not a "they" but a "we"—devout and dedicated clergy and laity.

Moberly, Elizabeth. *Homosexuality: A New Christian Ethic.* James Clarke & Co. Available in 1993 through Regeneration Books, P.O. Box 9830, Baltimore, Maryland 21284-9830. Conservative perspective on root causes of homosexuality and how they can be healed.

Morris, Calvin. "The Images and Likeness of God." *Sojourners,* July 1991. pp. 27-28. African-American pastoral care professor emphasizes the inclusiveness of Christ's love, warning against using the Bible to oppress gays and lesbians.

O'Neill, Craig, and Kathleen Ritter. *Coming Out Within.* San Francisco: Harper & Row, 1992. A spiritual exploration into issues of loss.

Seamands, David A. *Healing for Damaged Emotions.* Wheaton, Ill.: Scripture Press. Available in 1993 through Regeneration Books, P.O. Box 9830, Baltimore, Maryland 21284-9830. Demonstrates God's healing power to help break chains from one's past.

CHAPTER 8

WEAVING A THEOLOGY OF HOMOSEXUALITY

Donald E. Messer

Chapter 8

Over the centuries, Christians have responded in different ways when they have woven their theologies of homosexuality. Caught in the crossfire of debate over homosexuality, four types of theological responses have emerged from Christians.[1] The "rejecting-punitive" approach does not appear in the thinking of any writer in this book or any major contemporary Christian theologian. However, this attitude or approach does manifest itself in the public and church domains, as persons reject homosexuality as unchristian and express a punitive approach to gay and lesbian persons. Historically, stoning, burning, sexual mutilation, and even the death penalty have been justified on this basis.

The second type, "rejecting-nonpunitive" position, condemns homosexuality but not the homosexual person. God does not approve same-sex relationships, and the fullness of God's creation is achieved only through male-female marriages, but God's overwhelming grace is for everyone.

"Qualified acceptance," the third position, accepts the probability that sexual orientation is unlikely to be changed, so heterosexual Christians should be accepting and understanding but still maintain that homosexuality is a sin and celibacy is God's expected standard.

Variations of these two types of theological arguments appear in the writings of the more conservative authors in this book and represent the standard position of most mainline Protestant churches and the Roman Catholic church.

"Full acceptance" characterizes the fourth position. Persons holding this view, says James B. Nelson, "most often make the assumption that the homosexual orientation is more of a given than a free choice. More fundamentally, however, this position rests on the conviction that same-sex relationships can richly express and be the vehicle of God's humanizing intentions."[2] The more liberal authors in this book, clearly representing the minority opinion within the church, advocate "full acceptance" and reflect a belief that Christian love demands no less.

Doing Theology Every Day

These four types provide guidance to the individual believer, but what remains critical for the individual person in the pew is, What do I believe as a Christian about homosexuality? In reality Christians "do theology" every day. Theological reflection is not the exclusive professional prerogative of the clergy or the seminary faculty. For that matter, it doesn't belong solely to persons elected to church conferences. All of us make choices and act in certain ways because of the way we think theologically.

At the Harvard Business School, professors insist that the only effective way to learn business and economic theory is to study realistic case situations encountered in the real world. Similarly, ethicists emphasize that abstract theoretical perspectives have meaning or relevance only when applied to difficult, if not decisive, case issues like abortion, bioethics, war, or peace. Likewise, the challenge to Christians is to relate their theology to daily existence, abiding beliefs, guiding principles, and concrete actions. Christians find it particularly difficult and demanding to relate their theology to their understanding of sexuality, particularly homosexuality.

To think theologically is to appropriate the resources of our faith in reflecting on real-life dilemmas and situations. The Pauline Epistles illustrate how Paul thought theologically about real-life questions. As New Testament scholar Krister Stendahl has noted, "Paul did not write general theology to a general reader; he drew on the resources of his theological experience and tradition to address and illumine particular problems for a particular group of people."[3] For example, in his first letter to the church in Corinth, he gave theological advice for Christians struggling with controversial issues such as the division of loyalties within the church, immorality, and the proper use of "spiritual gifts."

At times, of course, our behavior betrays our beliefs, since human beings have a propensity for not practicing what we preach. Even apostles, like Paul, declared, "For I do not do the good I want, but the evil I do not want is what I do" (Rom. 7:19). This disjuncture between values and behavior has long been recognized by sociologists and others. Gunnar Myrdal identified the "American Dilemma" that despite the public profession of equality and justice, historic segregation and contemporary racism persisted.[4] For Christians, reconciling values and behavior remains a continuing dilemma, especially in regard to homosexuality. For conservatives, commitments to love and justice are often lost in condemning homosexual practices. For liberals, acceptance and understanding often seem to overshadow a willingness to set boundaries on what is or is not acceptable Christian behavior.

Realizing that some people think their way into new ways of acting, while possibly more people act their way into new ways of thinking, it remains essential that theology develop in response to empirical or actual situations.[5] Knowing personally people who are gay or lesbian may help one discover new scriptural insights and resources. Exploring one's own experiences, either negative or positive in regard to homosexuality, and examining one's own sexuality may make a difference in how one thinks about issues such as lifetime celibacy, ordination, or same-sex unions.

Deeply religious parents discovered their son was gay. The theology they embraced taught them that homosexuality equated with being a "sinner." For them, that meant rejecting their son and his sexual behavior. Sometime later the parents belatedly learned their son had AIDS. At the very moment their child needed his parents' love, and they felt a need to give it, theology stood blocking the doorway of their hearts. To compound the tragedy, the parents felt they could not share their pain with their pastor or congregation because they feared only condemnation, and not compassion, would be the response.

If the authors in this book were to confront this actual case history, they all would contend that the parents did not respond appropriately and the church has failed to be the true Body of Christ. Does anyone believe God ever intended parents not to love their children? Treating gays and lesbians as nonpersons, like the lepers of biblical times and the untouchables of India, is completely contrary to the gospel of Jesus Christ.

The Kroegers, Looney, Case, Dawn, and Nicolosi are likely to counsel that Christians should "hate the sin but love the sinner." Christians can never reject a child of God, but loving a person does not require approving or accepting objectionable behavior. Writing in an evangelical periodical, Stanton L. Jones asks fellow conservatives to "exhibit the love and compassion of Jesus Christ," saying that "revulsion to an act is not the same as a revulsion to a person. If you cannot empathize with a homosexual person because of fear or revulsion, then you are failing our Lord."[6]

On the other hand, authors Fuller, Furnish, Nelson, Sample, Glaser, and Graham would assert that the parents had embraced an exclusive, rather than inclusive, Christian faith. A faith that denies a person's sexual identity, and labels even the most positive expression of that identity as sin, cannot really be loving. The parents, pastor, and congregation demonstrate the scriptural teaching that inhospitality represents a most grievous sin worthy of condemnation.

All Christians would affirm that life in Christ ought to be a wonderful, joyful, life-fulfilling experience. To be a Christian is to soar in the spirit, to have wings that lift us beyond, to fly with the angels of grace and mercy. Unfortunately, for many persons their Christian theology is a shackle that locks their hearts, imprisons their minds, chains their souls, and tortures their bodies. Instead of freedom in Christ, they know only slavery. Instead of possessing a theology that fits their life experiences, they discover their belief system is dysfunctional to life.

Whether we are liberal or conservative or somewhere in between, how we think or act theologically may be revealed, for example, by asking ourselves some basic questions. Do our thoughts about God hinder or help us in loving other persons? Does the way we read the Bible obscure or open our vision of God's truth? Do the traditions and teaching of our church freeze us in the past or free us for the future? Does our Christian faith contradict or correspond to what we experience in life? Does our theology limit or liberate us in the way we respond to people and the kind of world in which we live? Do our beliefs create barriers or draw us closer to other children of God?

Weaving a Theology of Homosexuality

The art of weaving serves as a fitting image of how Christians do theology in daily life. Like weavers, we mingle together different threads of human experience and faith perspective into the colorful fabric we call existence. Most persons do not think theologically by simply making deductions from abstract principles or propositions, but instead reflect and respond to various fibers of faith, "uniting and integrating separate strands into an interwoven whole."[7] Using the weaving metaphor, let us examine how persons create a theology of homosexuality on the loom of life.

For perhaps twenty thousand years, weavers around the world have understood the loom as their most important tool. It is the basic structure on which weaving takes place. Its major function has been to keep "attractive rows of warp threads stretched to an even tension, like so many violin strings."[8] The vertical warp strands run lengthwise on the loom as a shuttle is passed through them carrying the horizontal weft threads. Out of these basic materials, a woven fabric emerges, thanks to the creative skill, patience, design, and imagination of the weaver. Whether one sees an African creating a basket, a Guatemalan weaving a fabric, a Native American constructing a rug, a cowboy braiding rope, or a spider spinning a web, one cannot help being awed by the beauty and the mystery of the artistry.

So it is when creating theology—one seeks to harmonize the interlocking warp threads of Scripture, tradition, experience, and reason with the weft strands of doctrine such as God the creator, human nature and sin, grace and Jesus Christ, the church and ministry. No one is required to spin a theological perspective on homosexuality that is identical with any of the authors represented in this book. Persons don't have to align themselves with one school or another, but they can weave their own pattern with integrity and beauty. The hope is that what materializes from one's thought as a theological weaver will connect values with behavior as well as reflect divine mystery.

The Warp Threads of Theology

In formulating one's theology of homosexuality, Christians begin at various points and draw on a variety of sources. Whether one begins with reflection on a Bible passage or from a personal experience, the warp threads from all four major authoritative foundations of theology—Scripture, tradition, experience, and reason—need to be woven together if life and faith are to be meaningful and we are to discover the whole fabric of God's revelation.[9]

Christians must constantly struggle with correlating the gospel message with human existence. Inevitably in struggling with Scripture, tradition, experience, and reason, individuals tend to give different weight or more credence to one dimension than another. Evangelical theologian Clark H. Pinnock observes that evangelical or conservative Christians typically emphasize the traditional gospel message, while liberal Christians tend to focus on human realities and needs, "but both are really interested in correlating and integrating both dimensions. Each of them cares deeply about fidelity to the original message and creativity in the face of fresh challenges."[10]

Examining the essays in this book reinforces Pinnock's perspective; those who reject homosexual practices as incompatible with Christian faith and ethics typically stress a conservative interpretation of Scripture and tradition in connection to experience, while those more open to homosexual relationships read Scripture and even tradition differently as they link faith to experience. All take the Bible and Christian teachings seriously, but they often reach radically different conclusions as to their meaning and value today.

Scripture

Christians generally would view the Bible as the primary warp thread for theology. However, because of sharply differing understandings and interpretations, this strand fashions dramatically distinct designs in various theological weavings. A primary point of departure in how Christians think theologically about homosexuality stems from this fundamental disagreement. Chapter 2 in this book illustrates this acute divergence, as Richard and Catherine Clark Kroeger and Victor Paul Furnish present contrasting scholarly findings as to what the Bible says about homosexuality. Their disagreements illustrate M. Kent Millard's warning that

> it must be recognized that equally sincere Christians may disagree as to which insights from the Bible should be applied to a particular social issue and they might further disagree about the nature of Biblical authority and how the Bible ought to be interpreted and applied to social concerns. Consequently, . . . one must recognize one's own presuppositions in interpreting the Bible and the basis on which one chooses Biblical passages to inform thinking.[11]

For example, the conservative case against homosexuality often rests on a particular way of understanding the authority and primacy of the Bible. God's truth is what Scripture says; what is written in the Bible becomes binding on the Christian. Not only the seven particular passages in Scripture that refer to homosexuality are interpreted as condemning its practice, but the totality of the Bible is understood as being supportive only of heterosexual relationships. If one adopts this approach to theology, disagreeing with or contradicting what the Bible is interpreted as saying proves impossible.

Critics of doing theology in the conservative fashion contend that such an approach necessitates an incredible mental gymnastic that both defies and denies God's continuing revelation through tradition, experience, and reason. An alternative approach to doing theology recognizes that the Bible is not independent from its interpreters. (Scripture did not suddenly appear in a bound volume, but results from centuries of conscientious religious persons seeking to understand and interpret God's will and way for humanity.) Written in different languages from our own, the Bible has been conditioned by historical, social, and scientific understandings distinct from those of the contemporary world.

Material within the New Testament directly related to homosexuality is quite limited. No record exists of Jesus' encountering or relating in any way to homosexual persons. Fred Craddock has noted the silence of Jesus on this subject, but he warns that this silence cannot be used to justify any particular stance on the subject, since "silence is simply silence. All we can conclude is that, as far as we know, any struggling by early Christians with the issues of homosexuality proceeded without a saying from the Lord."[12]

Tradition

The thread of tradition basically refers to what the church has taught over the centuries. Since Christians have often disagreed on many issues, this might more accurately be identified as "traditions" rather than "tradition." Inevitably, we are tempted selectively to retrieve only those strands of historical teaching, doctrine, or practice that reinforce our preferred stance.

Until recently, the overwhelming evidence emerging from tradition expressed anathema to same-sex relationships. Churches of Roman Catholic, Protestant, and Orthodox backgrounds have favored prohibitions and proscriptions against homosexuality. Traditional arguments have varied over time, sometimes reflecting a concern for lack of procreation and/or expressing a patriarchal viewpoint. The witness of early church fathers like John Chrysostom, Augustine, and Thomas Aquinas against homosexuality is well known, as are the views of Martin Luther, John Calvin, and Karl Barth. Lost in the transmission have been voices and documents from church history demonstrating the possibilities of tolerance or acceptance of gay and lesbian persons and practices. Yale historian John Boswell, however, has begun to discover forgotten traditions that call into question this uniform condemnation, and he suggests that the church at various periods of history was more open to gays and lesbians in the leadership of the church and at times blessed same-sex unions or marriages.

Attention to the diversity within tradition prompts us to examine critically our own knowledge of Christian faith and practice. Being human, and subject to sin, none of us can claim absolute understanding of the mystery of God's will. Likeside, none of us has complete mastery of what other Christians in other times and places have experienced, thought, and written. We are constantly challenged to engage in a dialogue with other Christian witnesses such as Mark, Luke, Paul, Francis of Assisi, Sojourner Truth, Albert Schweitzer, Martin Luther King, Jr., and Mother Teresa that we might discover what it meant and what it means to be a Christian.

Experience

Just as value is gained by learning from the experience of past Christians, it is likewise imperative we be open to our own experiences. If we dare to make judgments regarding the sexuality of others, we must be open to listening to and evaluating the experiences of Christian gays and lesbians, as well as ex-gays and ex-lesbians. Their personal stories are included in chapter 1 and elsewhere, lest this book be an impersonal, theoretical debate about issues that in reality reflect great struggle, pain, courage, and hope.

The warp strand of experience in theology, of course, is

broader than stories or personal feelings. It includes the data and information now available via the natural and social sciences. In weaving a theological picture of what we believe regarding homosexuality, the importance of being scrupulously honest in gathering factual data cannot be overstated. Since knowledge tends to be incomplete, limited, and socially conditioned, a certain humility about making absolute assertions should guide the Christian.

Using the best knowledge available was illustrated by H. Richard Niebuhr when he pointed out that "the Christ who commended a good Samaritan for pouring oil and wine into wounds would scarcely likewise honor a man who, trained in contemporary methods of giving first aid, regarded the Biblical example as his absolute guide."[13] Thus in approaching the subject of homosexuality, Ruth L. Fuller and Joseph Nicolosi have sought in their chapter on what science teaches to present as accurately as possible the findings of the social and natural sciences regarding the complexities of homosexuality. Christian thinking is not frozen factually in another historical time zone; it honestly probes points of scientific consensus and areas of disagreement.

Reason

Jesus came to take away our sins, not our minds. The God-given gift of reasoning completes the vertical warp strands on the loom of life. Whenever reason is absent from religion, the possibilities for irrationality, contradiction, and inconsistency flourish. Theologian Delwin Brown contends that if one believes in a God still active in human affairs, "might we not learn something from God through reason?"[14] Reason represents another form of God's continuing revelation for humanity, guarding against possible flaws imbedded in tradition and experience and Scripture. Because reason likewise runs the risk of being perverted by human sin, each strand criticizes as well as complements the other. A theology woven solely on the basis of reason would seriously lack the dimension and mystery required in a Christian fabric of faith.

Although Christians generally affirm the primacy of Scripture, that does not mean abandoning the insights of experience, the wisdom of tradition, or the critical analyses of reason. Reason, for example, requires us to be honest about the human condition. Christians are not required to pretend they live in an Alice-in-Wonderland world where they have to believe "as many as six impossible things before breakfast."[15] Rather, they are required to give critical and creative reflection on all four theological sources, seeking to be faithful interpreters and doers of God's Word in contemporary times.

All four warp threads of theology are indispensable for Christians. Appealing to Scripture alone for guidance proves impossible; thus the need to relate Christian tradition, reason, and experience to the biblical revelation. The theological debate whether homosexuality can be characterized as sinful, for example, necessitates an exploration of many basic Christian assumptions and beliefs about God's creation, human nature, and divine grace. Determining whether Christianity and the practice of homosexuality are incompatible requires both an exploration of Christian tradition and an investigation of basic Christian teachings. Questions such as whether homosexual persons should be ordained and whether the church should affirm covenantal unions for gay and lesbian persons dictate a careful analysis of topics such as the meaning of "call" and ordination and marriage. The theological and ecclesiastical rationales for restrictions need to be articulated along with the arguments used to challenge these limitations. No single person probably has enough theological information on any of the topics, but we must be open to learning from others and discerning the will of God in these matters.

The Weft Strands of Theology

Certain theological themes dominate Christian thinking about homosexuality. By examining divergent ways authors in this book have treated these weft strands or subjects, readers can ferret out various assumptions and prayerfully decide what they believe and where they stand on critical issues. Obviously, a variety of colorful theological strands could be used for this analysis, but for purposes of this discussion, let us highlight four spiritual strings central to every fabric of faith.

God the Creator

Christians of all theological persuasions are united in affirming God as creator. Most would also assert that sexuality is a good and gracious gift of God. But beyond that agreement, Christians tend to disagree sharply, especially in regard to homosexuality. When they weave their theologies of homosexuality, they display a distinctively different design from one another.

Probably the foremost and most fundamental question posed is whether being gay or lesbian is a matter of choice or a mode of creation. When people speak of sexual preference, they generally are asserting that sexuality is a matter of self-selection. If persons talk of sexual orientation, they may still mean choice, or they may believe that the causes of homosexuality are basically beyond the realm of conscious decision making.

First, let us look at the strands that compose the theology conservative Christians spin. Remember, however, that not all persons who assert that homosexual practice is incompatible with Christian faith share the exact theological and biblical assumptions. While similarities exist in the texture of their theology, they may differ significantly in regard to particular designs.

Conservatives who speak of homosexuality as "unnatural" or "contrary to God's intended plan" believe people were not created that way by God. Or they view homosexuality as a "flaw" in creation or a sinful result of "the Fall" that needs repentance and correction. Thus, Riley B. Case emphasizes the power of prevenient, justifying, and sanctifying grace to overcome the sin of homosexuality. Generally, persons who affirm traditional views reject theories that advocate a genetic or constitutional basis for homosexuality. They dispute findings and claims suggesting that people may be born predisposed to a sexual life as a gay or lesbian. A basic belief is that persons can choose a heterosexual life-style or refrain from expressing their homosexual inclinations. Though Joseph Nicolosi acknowledges that nature and nurture are so tightly woven together that the etiology of homosexuality is nearly impossible to unravel, he yet asserts that people are not born gay and points to the possibility of "reparative therapy" for those who choose to depart from a gay life-style. God did not deliberately create gay and lesbian persons. Authors like Richard and Catherine Clark Kroeger cite biblical texts, arguing that the Creation stories and scriptural references to marriage clearly specify relations between man and woman, not between persons of the same sex.

On the other hand, woven into the theological tapestry of Christians who affirm same-sex relationships is the conviction that God the creator allows variation in the creation of human personalities. The Old Testament stories of Creation are not mistaken for scientific explanations but are considered profound poetic expressions of faith, affirming God's good and creative powers. As Victor Furnish notes, the patriarchal and cultural biases of ancient biblical days cannot be given normative authority over contemporary Christians.

James Nelson and others would point to the discrepancy in the way the Bible is interpreted in regard to divorce versus homosexuality. Though Jesus apparently opposed divorce in three of the Gospels, and theologians opposed divorce for the first seventeen hundred years of Christian history, both conservative and liberal Christians have now adopted a more humane and understanding stance on this issue. Yet when faced with homosexuality, a subject on which Jesus was not known to have said anything, often Christians suddenly become biblical literalists when they interpet seven scattered biblical passages regarding certain homosexual practices. Why does it seem common for sermons to dwell on the love and parables of Jesus until the subject of homosexuality arises and then often preachers start quoting Leviticus?

For more liberal Christians, whether homosexuality is due to genetics and/or due to socialization in early years of life remains basically immaterial. Sexuality—be it heterosexuality or homosexuality—is more of a gift given of God than a matter of personal choice. Years ago Bishop Melvin E. Wheatley noted,

> Homosexuality, quite like heterosexuality, is neither a virtue nor an accomplishment. It is a mysterious gift of God's grace communicated through an exceedingly complex set of chemical, biological, chromosomal, hormonal, environmental, developmental factors totally outside my homosexual friend's control. His or her homosexuality is a gift—neither a virtue nor a sin. What she/he does with their homosexuality, however, is their personal, moral, and spiritual responsibility. Their behavior as a homosexual may therefore be very sinful—brutal, exploitative, selfish, promiscuous, superficial. Their behavior on the other hand, may be beautiful—tender, considerate, loyal, other-centered, profound.[16]

Human Nature and Sin

Bishop Wheatley's perspective that homosexuality is a gift of God's grace stands in striking contrast to the perspective of persons who would equate homosexuality with sin. Woven into the conservative theological textile is Bishop Richard L. Looney's argument that homosexual practice is a "shameful act against nature" and a "distortion of God's norm." Evangelical theologian Clark H. Pinnock contends that the Scripture teaches and experience confirms that "God's positive will for human beings is heterosexuality and that homosexuality of any sort (whether inversion or perversion, whether exploitive or nonexploitive) falls outside his express will." In contrast, liberal theologian Delwin Brown believes that "certain forms of homosexual relationships are 'natural' for some people. . . . They are wholesome, enriching to the participants, committed, and consistent with God's will for their lives."[17]

Fundamental to Christian theology is that all persons are sinners and fall short of the glory of God. Perhaps nothing divides conservative and liberal Christians more on the issue of homosexuality than this question of human nature and sin. If God has created a significant percentage of persons with a homosexual orientation, how can this be identified as sin? Yet if the Bible is interpreted as condemning homosexual practices as sinful, how can Christians not so label them?

The weft strands dominant in the theology design of conservative Christians stress the biblical references to sinfulness of homosexual practices. Specific citations from the Bible are fundamental to this perspective, but a scriptural understanding that God created man and woman for each other remains no less important: Adam and Eve, not Adam and Steve! Conservative Christians also draw on experience as a theological resource, being appalled by reported stories and studies of promiscuous and perverted sexual activities particularly among some male homosexual persons.[18] Such activities violate God's creational design, prove harmful to individuals and the community, and weaken the family structure. The more conservative writers in this book would underscore that individual homosexual acts, while sinful, do not deserve to be placed in a uniquely negative category. They note Bible passages that also condemn some heterosexual practices, greed, pride, jealousy, and a host of other deadly sins. Whether such a generosity of spirit pervades the wider coinservative community remains problematic.

The church's general reluctance to acknowledge and address the systemic sin of historic and contemporary injustice perpetuated against homosexual persons especially upsets more liberal Christians. Why focus so much on individual acts or get so troubled by outrageous public behavior at a gay or lesbian pride parade, and yet ignore cultural and structural sin and oppression directed toward homosexual persons? Why hasn't the church been more active protesting violence against gays and lesbians?

A constructive theology of homosexuality needs to recognize that gays and lesbians are not only sinners, like the rest of humanity, but also the "sinned against" to use the terminology of evangelist Raymond Fung. The conquistadors in the Americas and the Holocaust in Europe epitomize how they were "sinned against." The literature of the conquest of the Americas after Christopher Columbus repeatedly justified genocide of the indigenous people because they allegedly were infidels, idol worshipers, and sodomites. The conquerors absolved themselves of the massacre of millions by claiming they were wiping out native peoples in the same way their God had dealt with the people of Sodom.[19] When Allied troops liberated the concentration camps, they freed Jews, gypsies, political prisoners, and others. But, unbelievably, they continued to imprison gays and lesbians—the persecution continued even after the Nazis were defeated![20]

The physical and psychological violence perpetuated against gays and lesbians, with the silence if not the blessing of the church, cannot easily be dismissed or ignored. In appealing to tradition as a criterion for theological reflection, one must remember the negative side of Christian history and how homosexual persons have been treated as nonpersons, denied civil rights, marginalized within the society, and victimized by hateful remarks and hurtful comments. Gay bashing is not a new phenomenon, but a practice long tolerated by the Christian church and modern society.

Mark Bowman contends that the questions typically debated in the church are: "Is homosexuality a sin? Can you be a Christian and homosexual?" He says that the queries should be: "Can you be a Christian and exclude people from the church? Is it a sin to be homophobic?"[21] How one answers these four questions helps clarify one's theological position regarding homosexuality.

Highly debated is the question whether persons with a homosexual orientation can and should change. Situationally prompted homosexuality (such as sometimes occurs in prison) has a higher record of reversal once the conditions change. Many Christian gay and lesbian persons testify that at points in their lives, they have sincerely sought to change their sexual orientation. Hours have been spent praying, going forward at revivals or healing services, or undergoing psychological therapy. Some have entered marriage believing it would resolve their sexual dilemma. Except for those who identify themselves as ex-gays, the witness of others is that attempts to change their orientation resulted in frustration and/or failure.

Psychiatrist Ruth L. Fuller speaks of the limited possibilities for change and the predominant professional psychological perspective that learning to accept one's orientation is usually a healthier response. In contrast, psychologist Joseph Nicolosi objects to what he characterizes as militant gay-for-life-and-loving-it pressure and politics, saying that reparative therapy can enable change in homosexual persons.

Closely related is the question of how persons should express their sexuality. Many churches take the stance that if individuals have a homosexual orientation, they should pledge themselves to a life of chastity or celibacy. This position is reflected in writings by Bishop Richard C. Looney, Richard and Catherine Clark Kroeger, Riley B. Case, and Marva J. Dawn. Dawn considers such sacrifice and even suffering as being virtuous. Other authors such as Tex Sample, Victor Paul Furnish, and James B. Nelson raise probing questions as to the appropriateness of such advocacy, suggesting that human sexuality is far more complex than conservative writers describe it.

Celibacy in Christian tradition has always been viewed as a unique theological gift, not an inborn trait, given to a few for the sake of the Kingdom, not a realistic pattern of behavior for the many. Roman Catholics have developed spiritual disciplines for persons devoting their lives to religious orders to aid in their struggle for celibacy; Protestants have often simply prescribed it as a moral law. Richard J. Foster urges the church to surround homosexual persons "with earnest prayer that they can be faithful to their calling of celibacy."[22]

But is giving up sexual expression for fifty years or more really what God wills for persons who experience a homosexual orientation? Are heterosexual persons demanding that gays and lesbians meet a standard that straights often neither believe nor honor themselves in practice? Championing involuntary celibacy for gays and lesbians seems to deny them their God-given rights for sexual love, intimacy, and security.

John J. McNeill contends that "only a sadistic God would create millions of humans as gay with no choice in the matter and no hope of changing and then deny them the right to express their gayness in a loving relationship for the rest of their lives under the threat of eternal damnation."[23] Yes, how one views human nature and sin has a fundamental impact on how one thinks theologically about homosexuality.

Grace and Jesus Christ

In fact, the picture of Jesus the Christ embroidered in the pattern of one's theological weaving is influenced significantly by how one understands sin in relation to homosexuality. For those who deem homosexual practice as evidence of the human fall from God's intention and grace, Jesus appears on the loom of life preaching repentance before being accepted into the kingdom or realm of God. The love of Jesus is interpreted as warning persons to refrain from same-sex activities and offering gays and lesbians the healing power of transformative grace. How attractive this portrait of Jesus as judge may be remains irrelevant to the conservative Christian who firmly believes that no other option reflects biblical and theological truth. Conservatives insist that truth and standards must be maintained regardless how painful or unpopular.

Repentance opens the gateway to the holy living of God's kingdom or realm. To suggest otherwise is to preach a "cheap grace" in which people are welcomed into the Kingdom without renouncing their sin. Yes, all people are sinners, but Christians cannot condone homosexual practices any more than they can sanction fornication, adultery, racism, or other specific actions contrary to the will of God.[24] Sketched in the corner of the weaving might be these words of Jesus: "Enter through the narrow gate; for the gate is wide and the road is easy that leads to destruction, and there are many who take it. For the gate is narrow and the road is hard that leads to life, and there are few who find it" (Matt. 7:13-14).

In the theological materials of those who do not equate sin with all homosexual practice, the weft strands compose a dramatically different image of Jesus the Christ. Woven into their thinking is a vision of Jesus as friend, accepting all into the kingdom or realm of God who have been marginalized and oppressed.[25] The centrality of Jesus' teaching regarding the Kingdom manifests itself, for example, in Tex Sample's argument that faithfulness to the realm of God ought to be the basic criterion determining whether homosexual persons should be ordained or not. He endorses gay and lesbian ordinations if the persons demonstrate they are living in faithful, loving, and monogamous same-sex unions.

Jesus as the incarnation of God's love does not demand the renunciation of one's basic sexuality, but he calls people to repentance from lives lacking fidelity, care, compassion, and other-centeredness. "Agape," self-giving love or grace, not only reflects the nature of God but stands as the Christian norm of behavior for all human relationships. Knit on the edge of their weaving might be Jesus' words: "This is my commandment, that you love one another as I have loved you. No one has greater love than this, to lay down one's life for one's friends. You are my friends if you do what I command you" (John 15:12-14).

If Jesus ever said anything about homosexuality, it is not recorded in the Bible. He did, however, speak extensively on God's unconditional love. Yet instead of dwelling on biblical texts or parables that accent your neighbor, Christians have historically been more concerned to justify Leviticus or Paul's comments in Romans. Instead of focusing on the incredible injustice and hatred demonstrated by Christians and others toward gays and lesbians over the centuries, people appear more concerned about specific homosexual acts between consenting adults. As James B. Nelson notes, the Bible more clearly advocates a "love ethic" rather than a "sex ethic."

Conservative Christians would argue that the above weavings tend to distort their views. "There is no ethical complexity," writes David Seamands, "regarding sexual norms in the scriptures. The biblical norm is heterosexual, monogamous marriage."[26] They counter that liberal Christians have a tendency to overlook Jesus' strong affirmation of marriage between a man and a woman. While he may not have spoken explicitly about homosexuality, he did quote directly and positively from Genesis 2:24 that "a man shall leave his father and mother and be joined to his wife, and the two shall become one flesh. . . . Therefore what God has joined together, let no one separate" (Matt. 19:5-6). John Stott suggests evangelicals have erred in concentrating on the Leviticus and Pauline passages, when the "strongest argument" is that "Jesus endorsed the male/female union in marriage."[27]

Furthermore, conservatives strongly object to characterizations that they do not love gay and lesbian persons. Giving voice to this perspective, Bishop Looney says people "get tired of being labeled a homophobe, a fundamentalist, a gay-basher, and a literalist. . . . Love sometimes says, 'You are accepted but your behavior is inappropriate.' Love expects from us a response that sometimes rejects a behavior."[28] Far from being homophobes, fearful or hateful of homosexual persons, they seek to be caring and compassionate people. Thus, people like Richard and Catherine Clark Kroeger, who find Christianity and homosexuality incompatible, swim in freezing waters for more than a mile to raise funds to combat AIDS. Indiana pastor Riley B. Case argues for a church open to all, without condoning either the practice of homosexuality or the sins of homophobia. He believes you can uphold God's standards of "holy living" without becoming judgmental or self-righteous.

Church and Ministry

The fourth weft strand—the nature of the church and its ministry—distinguishes the theological pattern of one's thought. The heart of considerable controversy among Christians focuses on how these threads are stitched into one's credo regarding homosexuality. The tightly woven unity of the church—at local, denominational, and ecumenical levels—has come unraveled precisely at this point, during debates on questions such as ordination, blessing of same-sex unions, and so forth.

A persistent problem of using political terms like "liberal" and "conservative" is that people seldom fit such descriptions at all times and on all subjects. As Delwin Brown has noted, "The terms 'liberal' and 'conservative' represent approximate ends of a rough continuum rather than inflexible divisions."[29] Sometimes liberals are conservative on certain issues, and at other times conservatives proves to be liberals on other points. Illustrating this phenomenon, the National Council of the Churches of Christ in the U.S.A. (typically labeled as "liberal" on social justice issues) adopted a very conservative stance when it not only rejected membership for the predominantly gay and lesbian Universal Fellowship of the Metropolitan Community Churches but refused to grant the UFMCC even the "lowest" form of affiliation possible. Such "observer status" is granted to the North American Islamic Society, the American Jewish Committee, and the Unitarian Universalist Association, but gay and lesbian Christians are excluded by the mainline and orthodox denominations composing the so-called liberal National Council of Churches![30]

Generally, the more "liberal" or "mainline" denominations have supported the civil rights of gays and lesbians, while more "conservative" or evangelical churches have been less public in their support or worked in clear opposition to efforts to ensure homosexual rights or to remove so-called sodomy laws. With rare exceptions have any church leaders—"liberal" or "conservative"—supported efforts for the state to legally recognize same-sex marriages or partnerships. Even when proclaiming civil rights for gays and lesbians, most denominations have denied the possibility of equal rights within the church, especially in regard to the ordination of those who are practicing homosexual persons.

The warp strand of church tradition dominates debate about the church and its ministry. As Bishop Looney emphasizes, "The ordination of practicing homosexual persons is forbidden by the overwhelming majority of Christian denominations." The limited exceptions by the early 1990s included the United Church of Christ, the United Church of Canada, the Unitarian Universalist Association, and the Universal Fellowship of the Metropolitan Community Churches, along with Reform Judaism. Dissenters within many denominations would argue that tradition does not equal truth, believing that misinterpretations of Scripture and lack of scientific knowledge based on experience have contributed to this historical bias. James B. Nelson would note that the church's condemnation of gay and lesbian people has not been consistent throughout history, since during some centuries "there was no particular Christian antagonism toward homosexuality, and legal prohibitions were rare." Episcopal Bishop John Shelby Spong underscores forgotten church history, which includes homosexual persons who served as popes, archbishops, bishops, abbots, priests, and deacons.[31] How many closeted pastors and priests serve with distinction today remains unknown.

The authors in this book unanimously view the church as a compassionate community open to all persons regardless of sexual orientation. Larry Kent Graham and Riley B. Case present contrasting, but complementary, portraits of how the church can minister to gay and lesbian persons. Graham notes with agony how the church has failed to stand in solidarity with the suffering, while Case believes one can be caring while simultaneously condemning homosexual practice.

Not represented in these pages are those extremist points of view within the Christian community that would exclude persons from the sacraments or ministries of the church because of their same-sex practices. The degree of openness to gays and lesbians might differ considerably, however, in regard to questions such as church leadership positions, church school teachers, camp counselors, and so forth, depending on how persons view scientific and theological information regarding homosexuality. Marva J. Dawn expresses some anxiety about homosexual persons in certain role models, lest they influence the sexual identity of others, particularly students. Others would sharply question such perspectives, contending persons do not develop homosexuality anymore than one chooses to be heterosexual. No scientific proof exists that demonstrates that persons develop a sexual orientation (either heterosexual or homosexual) from the influence of a role model.

A future battleground of debate in the church probably lies in the area of same-sex marriages or unions. Even the language we use will probably be hotly disputed. Two Presbyterians, Chris Glaser and Catherine Clark Kroeger, have presented in this book contrasting scriptural and historical understandings as they have woven theological arguments, respectively, justifying and disavowing Christian covenantal ceremonies. Increased questions can be expected about church policies that permit the blessing of animals and houses but prohibit the blessing of persons of the same sex who desire to live in fidelity and love. Strong expressions of feelings can be anticipated by all persons who participate in this continued controversy within the church and society.

Lest we think such controversy is new to the church and its ministry, recall that John Wesley faced criticism in the 1780s when he championed the cause of a young man named Blair who had been imprisoned because he was found guilty of homosexual sodomy in England. Wesley was accused of a "lack of discretion in taking up so eagerly the cause of young Blair." How scandalous for the young Methodist movement to countenance such a man, whether he was guilty or not. As one critic wrote in his diary, "Whatever good they pretend it was highly imprudent and has given the occasion of terrible reflections."[32] No doubt some people in the church today will think a church study on homosexuality is likewise "imprudent" and will be "the occasion of terrible reflections."

Disagreeing in Love

At this stage in the church's debate on homosexuality, abundant evidence exists that conflict will not diminish because consensus has not emerged. Since all conscientious Christians have not reached the same conclusions, a key question will be whether the church can not only survive but thrive while disagreeing in love. As two British church leaders have written, "The test of Christian fellowship is not whether we can be together when all are agreed but whether our love for Christ can hold us together when deep differences of belief would drive us apart."[33]

Emotional and ill-informed comments and decisions regarding homosexuality have prompted Christians into actions that have misrepresented the Christian faith, have hurt persons and families, and have caused embarrassment for those who spoke or acted before fully understanding the facts or their faith. On the other extreme, notes M. Kent Millard, are "those Christians who experience the 'paralysis of analysis' and refuse to make a decision" regarding homosexuality because

> they want to have all the knowledge possible and perfect faith before they decide. Between these two extremes the Christian is called upon to make his or her own Christian decision with as much knowledge and faith as possible while realizing that their knowledge and faith will be always incomplete.[34]

Such decision making, however, is not simply individualistic, since Christians bear responsibilities for others. We love as persons in community. "Our decisions," says John D. Godsey, "ought not be made in lonely internal dialogue, but in the living dialogue of the self with other selves, for what is at stake is not our eternal happiness but our responsibility to God for our neighbor."[35]

The high probability of any open study process is that all persons will not be in agreement during the exploration of a living dialogue. Disagreement probably will be experienced even at concluding time. Therefore, the challenge facing the church is whether it can be a community that builds trust and affirms healing among those who may never be able to agree.

Some seem to prefer living in ideological and organizational ghettos and, therefore, seek to coerce others into believing the way they do or separating themselves or others from the group. Bishop Woodie W. White of Indiana, however, warns against losing our sense of Christian community and viewing "one another only as adversaries, not as brothers and sisters in Christ." He urges all persons to "drop their posture of self-righteousness and arrogance," remembering always that it is Christ's church and Christ alone must be its Lord. Bishop White argues,

"When Christ is given primacy in our meetings, on our agendas, and in our strategies, we will be drawn back to our common ground and true sense of community in Christ as a 'redeemed and redeeming fellowship.' "[36]

The fragmentation of the church in a politicized and pluralistic era may not be completely avoidable, but the church needs to strive to overcome the temptation to be nothing more than a collection of special interests. The world has plenty of models of politicized fragmentation. What the world needs for salvation, says Michael Kinnamon, "is the transforming proclamation of God's love that binds us into communities of active love, even with those with whom we disagree."[37] An honest, open, and forthright inquiry regarding homosexuality offers the church an opportunity to test its ability to witness to the world how "speaking the truth in love" can deepen, not divide, genuine community.

NOTES

1. See James B. Nelson, *Embodiment: An Approach to Sexuality and Christian Theology* (Minneapolis: Augsburg Publishing House, 1978), pp. 188-99.

2. Ibid., p. 197.

3. Krister Stendahl, in ibid., p. 19.

4. See Gunnar Myrdal, *An American Dilemma* (New York: Harper & Brothers, 1944), and Robert Wuthnow, *The Struggle for America's Soul: Evangelicals, Liberals, and Secularism* (Grand Rapids: Wm. B. Eerdmans Publishing Co., 1989), pp. 31-34.

5. See Donald E. Messer, *Contemporary Images of Christian Ministry* (Nashville: Abingdon Press, 1989), p. 181.

6. Stanton L. Jones, "The Loving Opposition: Speaking the Truth in a Climate of Hate," *Christianity Today*, July 19, 1993, pp. 24-25.

7. Christine M. Smith, *Weaving the Sermon: Preaching in a Feminist Perspective* (Louisville, Ky.: Westminster/John Knox Press, 1989), p. 21.

8. Osma Gallinger Tod, *The Joy of Handweaving* (New York: Dover, 1964), p. 71.

9. Robert Neville calls this the "four essential moments in the hermeneutical circle," in *A Theology Primer* (Albany: State University of New York Press, 1991), p. 15. See also Clark H. Pinnock and Delwin Brown, *Theologi-*

cal Crossfire: An Evangelical/Liberal Dialogue (Grand Rapids: Zondervan Publishing House, 1990), pp. 21-57.

10. Pinnock, *Theological Crossfire*, p. 11.

11. Millard, p. 25.

12. Fred Craddock, "How Does the New Testament Deal with the Issue of Homosexuality?" *Encounter* 40 (Summer 1979): 201.

13. H. Richard Niebuhr, *Christ and Culture* (New York: Harper & Row, 1951), p. 234.

14. Brown, *Theological Crossfire*, p. 56.

15. Quoting the White Queen in Lewis Carroll, *Through the Looking Glass*, in *The Annotated Alice* (New York: World, 1963), p. 251.

16. Excerpt from statement made by United Methodist Bishop Melvin E. Wheatley, Oct. 12, 1981, Denver, Colorado.

17. Pinnock and Brown, *Theological Crossfire*, pp. 111, 124.

18. See Jones, "Loving Opposition," p. 23.

19. Lucien Chauvin, "Homosexuality Used to Justify Genocide," *Latinamerica Press*, Oct. 1, 1992, p. 7.

20. See Heinz Heger, *The Men with the Pink Triangle*, trans. David Fernbach (Boston: Alyson Publications, 1980).

21. Mark Bowman quoted in Rick Smith, "Gay Methodist Tries to Change Church Debate," *The Gazette* (Cedar Rapids, Iowa), May 18, 1993, p. 1. See also the booklet "Is Homosexuality a Sin?" published by Federation Parents FLAG, P.O. Box 27605, Washington, D.C.

22. Richard J. Foster, "God's Gift of Sexuality," *Sojourners*, July 1975, p. 19.

23. John J. McNeill, *Taking a Chance on God: Liberating Theology for Gays, Lesbians, and Their Lovers, Families, and Friends* (Boston: Beacon Press, 1988), p. 38. See also John J. McNeill, "Homosexuality: Challenging the Church to Grow," *The Christian Century*, March 11, 1987, pp. 242-46.

24. For a conservative presentation on this subject, see Richard F. Lovelace, *Homosexuality and the Church* (Old Tappan, N.J.: Fleming H. Revell Co., 1978).

25. See Gary David Comstock, *Gay Theology Without Apology* (Cleveland: Pilgrim Press, 1993), pp. 98-100.

26. David Seamands, quoted in "Reflections on the Homosexuality Study," *Good News*, Jan-Feb. 1992, p. 7.

27. John Stott, quoted in an interview by Michael G. Maudlin, "John Stott Speaks Out," *Christianity Today*, Feb. 8, 1993, p. 38.

28. Bishop Richard C. Looney, quoted in "Homosexual Report Received and Referred," *Good News*, Jan.-Feb. 1992, p. 36.

29. Brown, *Theological Crossfire*, p. 156.

30. See Bruce W. Robbins, "UFMCC and NCC: Unity Over Justice?" *Christianity and Crisis*, Jan. 4, 1993, p. 425.

31. John Shelby Spong, "Understanding the Gay Reality," *The Christian Century*, Jan. 22, 1986, p. 62.

32. Thomas Wilson's diary cited in V. H. H. Green, *John Wesley* (Lanham, Md.: University Press of America, 1987), p. 32.

33. Kathleen Richardson and Brian E. Beck in a joint statement reported by Austin Carley, "British Methodists Divided Over Sexuality," *The United Methodist Reporter*, July 9, 1993.

34. Millard, pp. 27-28.

35. John D. Godsey, *The Promise of H. Richard Niebuhr* (Philadelphia: J. B. Lippincott, 1970), p. 94. Godsey is summarizing Niebuhr's position.

36. Woodie W. White, "Even in Politics, the Church Should Be Different," *The United Methodist Reporter*, July 1-8, 1992, p. 2.

37. Michael Kinnamon, "Restoring Mainline Trust: Disagreeing in Love," *The Christian Century*, July 1-8, 1992, p. 648.

STUDY GUIDE

Christians "do theology" every day, and these beliefs influence the way we relate to gay and lesbian persons. In this chapter the weaving analogy is used to demonstrate how the warp threads of Scripture, tradition, experience, and reason intertwine on the loom of life with the weft strands of God the creator, human nature and sin, grace and Jesus Christ, and the church and its ministry.

Each reader is encouraged to weave a theology of homosexuality, based on the critical understanding of these four sources of theology. Donald E. Messer helps untangle the various theological positions, both conservative and liberal, to discover the distinctive patterns that emerge.

Items for Reflection

1. Do you believe human sexuality is God's good gift?

2. In speaking of the four sources of theology, Christians often speak of the primacy of Scripture. Does that mean upholding what the Bible says, even if tradition, experience, and/or reason seem to contradict it?

3. Is sexual orientation a matter of choice or a mode of creation?

4. Mark Bowman says that traditionally the church has asked, "Is homosexuality a sin? Can you be a Christian and homosexual?" He suggests that the queries should be: "Can you be a Christian and exclude people from the church? Is it a sin to be homophobic?" How you answer these four questions helps clarify your theological position regarding homosexuality.

SUGGESTED RESOURCES

Comstock, Gary David. *Gay Theology Without Apology*. Cleveland: Pilgrim Press, 1993. Presents a gay liberation theology.

Linscheid, John, ed. "Christians and Homosexuality—A Discussion of Biblical and Ethical Issues." *The Other Side Magazine*, updated ed., 1990.

McNeill, John. *Taking a Chance on God: Liberating Theology for Gays, Lesbians, and Their Lovers, Families, and Friends*. Boston: Beacon Press, 1988. Argues that both tradition and Scripture support same-sex love and how a positive gay identity is compatible with Christian faith.

Smedes, Lewis B. *Sex for Christians: The Limits and Liberties of Sexual Living*. Grand Rapids: Wm. B. Eerdmans Publishing Co., 1976. A theology of sex affirming heterosexual marriage as the only true Christian expression of sexuality is offered in forthright language. A long and sensitive section on homosexuality is included.

APPENDIX A

Things the Church Can and Cannot Responsibly Teach

The 1992 General Conference authorized The United Methodist Publishing House to publish study materials on homosexuality based on the findings of the United Methodist Committee to Study Homosexuality. The following findings from the study committee might be helpful in your ministry.

Things the Church *Can* Teach About Homosexuality

• Homosexuality is best considered in the context of a more general Christian understanding of human sexuality.

• Human sexuality is God's good gift. Our fundamental attitude toward this gift should be more one of gratitude than of apprehension.

• Sexual expression is most profoundly human when it takes place in the context of a caring and committed relationship where each partner can be an expression of God's grace for the other.

• There are substantial numbers of persons of homosexual orientation within the church whose gifts and graces manifest the work of the Spirit among us.

• The specific causes of homosexual orientation remain unclear, although various scientific theories about this contribute to our overall understanding.

• It is a responsible expression of Christian ethics to advocate for those things which minimize the spread of sexually transmitted diseases and to support work towards adequate health care and research in these areas.

• The basic human rights of gay and lesbian persons should be protected by the church, and the general stigmatizing of such persons is inappropriate in a church which understands all its members to be sinners who live by the power of God's grace.

• In the church's own dialogue on this as well as other controversial issues, persons of conflicting viewpoints should respect one another, recognizing that before the mystery of God, our knowledge and insight remain partial and imperfect.

Things the Church *Cannot* Responsibly Teach About Homosexuality

• The church cannot teach that the Bible is indifferent to homosexual acts. Although there are only a few passages on the topic, in every one of those passages a negative judgment about homosexual practice is either stated or presumed.

• The church cannot teach that all biblical references and allusions to sexual practices are binding today just because they are in the Bible. Specific references and allusions must be examined in light of the basic biblical witness and their respective sociocultural contexts.

• The church cannot teach that certain sexual behaviors are morally acceptable just because they are practiced by substantial numbers of people, nor just because the acts correspond to subjective inclinations. Not all expressions of sexuality can be affirmed by the church as moral or life enhancing. This applies to both heterosexual and homosexual practices.

• The church cannot teach that gay and lesbian persons are generally dysfunctional or characteristically preoccupied with sex—some are and some are not.

• The church cannot teach that the same percentage of every society is gay or lesbian. This is not borne out in cross-cultural studies.

• The church cannot teach that sexual orientation is fixed before birth, nor can it teach that it is fixed only after birth. The scientific evidence is insufficient to allow a judgment either way.

• The church cannot teach that sexual orientation, either heterosexual or homosexual, is deliberately chosen. It is clear that substantial numbers of persons have experienced their sexual orientation from early childhood.

• The church cannot teach that there is a single theory of homosexual orientation or behavior.

• The church cannot affirm any sexual practice, heterosexual or homosexual, that is exploitative, casual, or physically threatening.

The United Methodist Newscope, vol. 20, no. 49, Dec. 11, 1992

APPENDIX B

What Is a "Self-Avowed Practicing Homosexual"?

United Methodist Legislation

The phrase "self-avowed practicing homosexual" was inserted in the 1984 *Discipline* of The United Methodist Church by action of the General Conference. A key paragraph (402.2) reads:

> While such persons set apart by the Church for the ministry of Word, Sacrament, and Order are subject to all the frailties of the human condition and pressures of society, they are required to maintain the highest standards represented by the practice of fidelity in marriage and celibacy in singleness. Since the practice of homosexuality is incompatible with Christian teaching, self-avowed practicing homosexuals are not to be accepted as candidates, ordained as ministers, or appointed to serve in The United Methodist Church.

The 1984 General Conference was not specific in its definitions. Responsibility for definition and interpretation rests with the Annual Conference. The Judicial Council has declared that:

> Because the legislation lacks specific definition regarding avowal and practice of homosexuality, and because of Methodism's long-standing and continuing principle that ministerial members of an Annual Conference shall receive an annual appointment (Par. 422, *1984 Discipline*), care must be taken in applying Par. 402.2 to follow due process, protecting the rights of ministerial members. The Annual Conference must make any determination which would effect a change in ministerial standing.[1]

In 1986 the Rocky Mountain United Methodist Conference endorsed the results of a ten-person committee of laity and clergy by adopting the definition set forth in this document and by accepting the commentary as operational guidelines for its deliberations. It is included in this book as an example of how the church responds when caught in the crossfire of debate regarding homosexuality.

Definition

The three words *self-avowed practicing homosexual* are not used as independent terms but as a phrase and must be so defined in that context. For purposes of a definition:

A self-avowed practicing homosexual is a person who engages in, and openly acknowledges, genital sexual behavior with a person or persons of the same sex.

Commentary

This definition emerged on the basis of extensive deliberations. Seven notes in particular proved important in making a decision as to definition:

1. *Understanding of Homosexuality.* The teachings and legislation of The United Methodist Church assume a model of homosexuality that distinguishes between orientation and acting upon that orientation. The Social Principles affirm "homosexual persons no less than heterosexual persons are individuals of sacred worth. All persons need the ministry and guidance of the Church in their struggles for human fulfillment, . . . "But the Social Principles also declare that The United Methodist Church does ". . . not condone the practice of homosexuality and considers this practice incompatible with Christian teaching. . . . "

2. *Practice, Not Orientation, Prohibited.* The question whether one is a homosexual person by orientation is irrelevant to the definition, as evidenced by the 1984 General Conference legislative debate and in decisions of the United Methodist Judicial Council.[2] It is therefore inappropriate to question a person's sexual orientation as a fitness standard for ministry.

The United Methodist Church does not exclude homosexually-oriented persons from the ordained ministry, but persons who openly acknowledge practicing that orientation are prohibited from being accepted as candidates, ordained as ministers, or appointed to serve.[3]

3. *Fidelity in Marriage and Celibacy in Singleness.* The normative sexual standard set forth by The United Methodist Church for ordained ministers, and candidates for ordination, is ". . . the practice of fidelity in marriage and celibacy in singleness." These terms were not defined by the General Conference. The United Methodist Church has no clear tradition or teaching regarding the vocation of celibacy. A United Church of Canada report defines "celibacy" as "the intentional decision to forego any expression of genital sexual activity with another person."[4]

4. *Self-avowed.* The term "self-avowed" means openly acknowledging both homosexual orientation and practice.[5] It was purposely inserted by the General Conference, presumably to avoid "witch-hunts" or harassment of persons within the church through implication or innuendo by emotionally accusing

persons and unduly invading the personal privacy of clergy or candidates for ordination.[6]

An effort was made at the General Conference to delete this term. It was argued that the inclusion of this term would be, in effect, to say that a person must self-avow, or openly acknowledge, one is a practicing homosexual. This effort to delete "self-avowed" was defeated overwhelmingly on a hand vote with no count taken.[7] Since it is clear from previous Judicial Council decisions that an Annual Conference cannot require (or in this case, prohibit) something General Conference has voted down, then the term "self-avowed" must be an integral part of any definition.[8]

Therefore, the "self-avowal" of homosexual orientation and behavior is necessary before a person can be prohibited from candidacy, ordination, or appointment within The United Methodist Church.

5. *Practicing.* A "practicing" homosexual is interpreted to refer to a person who engages in genital sexual behavior with a person or persons of the same sex. Recognizing a variety of cultural and contextual settings (e.g., hugging or kissing or even football players patting one another), the comprehensive possibilities of the term "practice" should be limited and used to refer solely to genital sexual behavior, differentiating it from casual demonstrations of affection between two persons of the same sex.

One critical dimension of the definition was left unresolved. The committee agreed to disagree on whether "practicing" implied habitual, consistent, or customary behavior in contrast to isolated, occasional, or experimental.

Some committee members felt that to include language such as "habitual" or "more than a single act" would imply the church's endorsement of even isolated actions, giving license to unacceptable behavior. Though there was no clear debate at General Conference on this term, it was believed that those who drafted this General Conference legislation did not intend to provide for such a possibility.

Others noted even the *Discipline* recognizes "the frailties of the human condition." Further, they insisted the General Conference meant for a literal definition of the word *practicing*, meaning "more than a single act" or "doing some act many times over." By definition *practicing* means "regularly" or "customarily."

6. *A Phrase Without a Comma.* Contrary to most news reports, in both the secular and church press, there is not a comma in the phrase "self-avowed practicing homosexual" as it appears in the *Book of Discipline.* If it were present, what difference would it make?

The judgment of the committee is that if there were a comma, there would be two separate questions: are you a self-avowed homosexual? and are you a practicing homosexual? Since there is no comma, the words "self-avowed" and "practicing" are used like adjectives to modify the noun, raising but one question: do you avow that you are a practicing homosexual?

If there were a comma, self-avowal would pertain only to the matter of acknowledging one's sexual orientation with the Board of Ordained Ministry determining sexual practice. The absence of a comma indicates that both orientation and practice are a matter for self-avowal, and it is neither necessary nor appropriate for the Board of Ordained Ministry to do anything more than to ascertain whether a person is a self-avowed practicing homosexual.

7. *Questioning Persons in a Covenantal Church.* In the twentieth century, the list of prohibited actions which clergy have been asked to pledge to avoid has included going to the theatre, dancing, drinking, playing cards, and smoking. Illustrative was the 1952 Methodist *Discipline* (321.4) which required ministers to answer affirmatively the question, "Are you willing to make a complete dedication of yourself to the highest ideals of the Christian ministry and bear witness to the same by your abstinence from the use of tobacco and other indulgences . . . ?" This style of examining and defining clergy morality was debated and discarded at the 1968 Uniting Conference.[9] While the 1984 General conference once again adopted a specific prohibition against self-avowed homosexual practice, it did not insert a question that must be answered in the affirmative.

Nevertheless, it seems appropriate in a covenantal church for ministerial candidates to be informed of the disciplinary standards of the church. Candidates for ministry are first approved and encouraged by local churches. In that setting or in District Committees, they could be asked: "Are you aware of the law of the church?" Consensus was that candidates should not be interrogated about their private lives but simply made aware of the law and expectations of the church for its ordained clergy. This could help to avoid later difficulties arising from a candidate's lack of knowledge concerning what is required by the 1984 legislation of The United Methodist Church.

Questions of this nature should be reserved to limited confidential settings, and only when formal charges have been brought. In such an instance, the Board of Ordained Ministry, or an appropriate investigative/trial body, might simply ask the accused person: "Are you a self-avowed practicing homosexual?" Critical to the process is the integrity and truthfulness of the person responding.

The committee discussed whether the avowal must occur within a particular place or forum and whether it could be proven by actions as opposed to words, spoken, written, or otherwise acknowledged by the accused person. Some members advocated a position that actions alone could constitute an avowal, but this position was not accepted by the group as a whole. There seemed to be consensus that the avowal need not be made during the investigation but could have been made by an individual outside the forum itself. Whether the avowal must nevertheless be made in a public setting as opposed to a private setting outside the forum involved was not determined by the committee.

The complexities and ambiguities of writing definitions in these matters need to be recognized. The committee urged against an excessively legalistic interpretation, and forms of questioning that invade unduly the privacy of persons. Let the church rely instead on a trusting, covenantal understanding of Christian ministry. The basis of this covenant is the personal conscience of each person. This is not perfect, but it is much to be preferred to a new church inquisition.

We cannot ignore the disciplinary law of the Church, even as we recognize the right for persons conscientiously to object to particular teachings. The

Church alone decides whom it shall set aside for the ordained ministry. Ordination is a church rite, not a civil right.

Above all, it cannot be overemphasized that the Church is a covenantal community and ours is a covenant ministry of grace. Let us never substitute the primacy of spiritual and moral attainment within our lives for the primacy of grace and faith offered as a free gift by a merciful God. The United Methodist Church does not understand itself as a community of a morally pure, but as laity and clergy standing equally in need of God's grace. Let all our relationships with one another be characterized by Christ's redemptive spirit, forgiving one another as God in Christ has forgiven us.

Notes

1. See Judicial Council #544. Also see *Daily Christian Advocate*, May 12, 1984, pp. 741-742.

Remember that the phrase prohibiting a "self-avowed practicing homosexual" was first defeated by a vote of 496 to 474 (51.1% to 48.9%). After the Judicial Council ruled that the phrase "fidelity in marriage and celibacy in singleness" would not necessarily preclude self-avowed practicing homosexuals from the ordained ministry, the General Conference reconsidered and passed this prohibition by a vote of 525 to 442 (54.2% to 45.8%).

2. In response to a question raised during the 1984 General Conference debate ("Could a self-avowed homosexual who is not a practicing homosexual be entitled to ordination?), Dr. David A. Seamands of Wilmore, Kentucky, replied, "Yes, they could, because this does not address the question of orientation. We're talking only about practice and behavior, the same as the Social Principles. I want to say that this petition that I have presented is basically the petition with a one-word editorial change which was sent by the Southeastern Jurisdiction Association of Conference Boards of Ministry." (*Daily Christian Advocate*, May 10, 1984, p. 638.)
The Concurring Opinion of Judicial Council Decision No. 544 declared that the 1984 legislation ". . . does not per se bar homosexual persons from the ordained ministry of The United Methodist Church.

3. The nature of the prohibited actions is addressed in item 5 of this commentary.

4. If the United Church of Canada definition were adopted, then celibacy becomes the practice of a determination to act in a certain way. In the case of The United Church of Canada this certain way would mean foregoing any expression of genital sexual activity; United Methodists might want to suggest it means foregoing any sexual intercourse. Celibacy thus becomes a matter of the will, or a vow, not a condition (such as presumably whether one is a "virgin" or not). What happens when this vow of celibacy is broken? Are there time boundaries within which an act must have occurred which would prohibit a person from candidacy, ordination, or appointment? What about the Christian understanding of forgiveness? These, and many other questions, are beyond the boundaries of this committee's assignment but not beyond the

realms of responsibility of those entrusted with the ordination process. This committee accepted the proposition that the sexual activity must be genital. The United Church of Canada references are from "Sexual Orientation and Eligibility for the Order of Ministry," Report of the Division of Ministry Personnel and Education on the Ordination and Commissioning of Self-Declared Homosexual Persons, 1984.

5. Despite the use of this term in official United Methodist circles since at least 1979, "self-avowed" did not appear in any of the dictionaries consulted by the Committee. Perhaps it is listed in one somewhere, but possibly it may be considered poor English in that it is redundant—"self" and "avowed" meaning one and the same thing.

6. The meaning of "openly" in this context is addressed in item 7 of this commentary.

7. Reverend Richard H. Timberlake of Knoxville, Tennessee, argued that ". . . the word 'self-avowed' weakens that language by saing, in effect, that a person must [sic] both be self-avowed and practicing. Our objective in this instance is not to deal with a person's nature or his avowal. It is to deal with his practice, and the intent of many of us who feel that the church must speak on this issue is to say that regardless of an individual's desires, wishes, feelings or inclination, that person must not practice homosexual acts. So I ask you to strike the word 'self-avowed' that we may strengthen the language of the amendment." (*Daily Christian Advocate*, May 12, 1984, p. 735.) One person spoke against the Timberlake Amendment; no one else spoke in favor of it.

8. The Judicial Council, in Decision #513, declared, ". . . an Annual Conference may not add nor subtract from the requirements established by the General Conference." In Decision #544 it declared that "While each Annual Conference is a door through which one may enter the ministry of the entire church, the Annual Conference cannot reduce nor avoid stipulations established by the General Conference which must be met by the church's ministry everywhere. An Annual Conference might set specific qualifications for its ministerial members, but does not have the authority to legislate in contradiction to a General Conference mandate or requirement."

9. See *General Conference Journal 1968*, p. 640.

INDEX

Scripture

Genesis

1–2 . . . . 49, 59, 142
19:1-25 . . . . 49, 59-60

Leviticus

18:22 . . . . 49, 60-61
20:13 . . . . 113, 134-35

Romans

1:26-27 . . 53, 61, 92, 113, 124, 126

2 Corinthians

6:9-10 . . 50, 51, 61, 113-114, 123, 26, 136-37

1 Timothy

1:8-11 . . . . 2, 61, 114, 123

Subjects and Authors